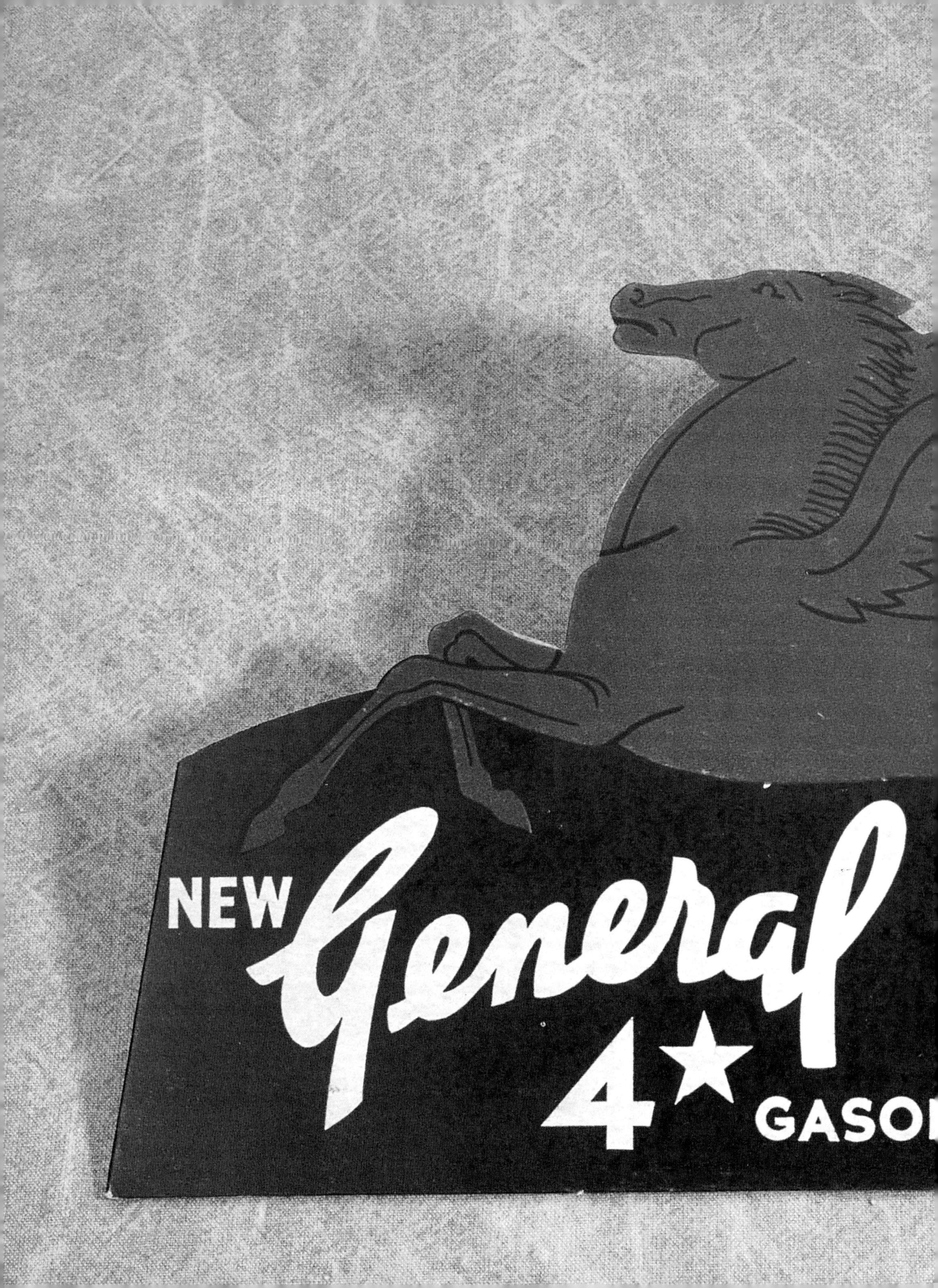
NEW
General
4★

Mobil
Collector's & Price Guide

Wayne Henderson & Scott Benjamin

MBI Publishing Company

PAT. APPLD. FOR

First published in 1998 by MBI Publishing Company, 729 Prospect Avenue, PO Box 1, Osceola, WI 54020-0001 USA

The information in this book is true and complete to the best of our knowledge. All recommendations are made without any guarantee on the part of the author or Publisher, who also disclaim any liability incurred in connection with the use of this data or specific details.

We recognize that some words, model names and designations, for example, mentioned herein are the property of the trademark holder. We use them for identification purposes only. This is not an official publication.

MBI Publishing Company books are also available at discounts in bulk quantity for industrial or sales-promotional use. For details write to Special Sales Manager at Motorbooks International Wholesalers & Distributors, 729 Prospect Avenue, Osceola, WI 54020-0001 USA.

Library of Congress Cataloging-in-Publication Data

Henderson, Wayne
    Mobil collector's & price guide / Wayne Henderson & Scott Benjamin .
        p. cm.
Includes index.
    ISBN 0-7603-0534-X (pbk. : alk. paper)
    1. Mobil Oil Company—Collectibles—Catalogs. 2. Service stations—collectibles—United States—Catalogs. 3. Petroleum industry and trade—Collectibles—United States—Catalogs.
I. Benjamin, Scott II. Title.
TL153.H463   1998
629.28'6'075—dc21   98-34414

On the front cover: Mobil's famous flying red horse adorned practically every object associated with the gas and oil company. Today, antique collectors and petroliana enthusiasts actively seek these wonderful items. Of particular interest are gas pump globes, porcelain signs, and lubricant containers.

On the frontispiece: Mobil manufactured hundreds of specialty lubricants for industrial applications worldwide. Many of the products were shipped in bulk and packaged locally, sold to end users in 5-gallon containers such as the one seen here.

On the title page: Mobil's Pegasus flew everywhere, even on the lubrication service attendant's cap! This is one of the more elaborate attendant hats ever used by a major oil company.

On the back cover: A great collection of Mobil collectibles, from the upper left: a toy gas station in the "drum" style architecture, a postwar oil can cabinet sign, a multiple-can oil rack complete with containers, and a Mobilgas Special three-piece glass gas pump globe.

Printed in Hong Kong through World Print, Ltd.

CONTENTS

ACKNOWLEDGMENTS

We would like to give special thanks to Dave Mercer for allowing us to photograph his extensive Mobil collection. Many of the items shown in this book are from Dave's collection, and we could not have accomplished this project without his help and generosity. For further information on Mobil collectibles, or if you have any Mobil items for sale, please contact Dave at 24007 Ventura Blvd., Suite 210, Calabasas, CA 91302 (818) 222–0301 or (818) 597–0388

We also thank Nick Cedar Photography and the other photograph contributors for providing beautiful illustrations and rare photographs.

—*Scott Benjamin and Wayne Henderson*

PREFACE

It was May of 1964 and I found myself with my parents on vacation in Huntington, West Virginia, visiting with friends who had recently moved there from my native Hampton, Virginia. I was excited, for during the visit I would be having my second birthday. Odd how some of us remember some things like this.

I remember we went downtown and into a huge store, one that I have since determined was the S. S. Kresge store that was operating there at that time. My parents and their friends selected gifts, and we returned home for cake and ice cream. I was sharing the birthday party with the daughter of the family we were visiting, who had turned two just the week before.

My parents have a photo of me sitting on the kitchen table, opening my presents. For my second birthday I received a Mobilgas toy tanker, much like one of those listed in this book, along with a Coca-Cola truck. The Mobilgas tanker stood out, however, because even at that age I had the fascination with gasoline stations that I still have today.

From that early experience, no doubt one that many children shared, I took my fascination on to much larger things. Think back...did you, perhaps, receive one of those toy Mobil trucks, too?

—*Wayne Henderson*

HOW TO USE THIS BOOK FOR REFERENCE

This book has been assembled in a format with which many readers will already be familiar. The listings are similar to those used in several of our earlier works, including *Gas Pump Globes, Oil Company Signs: A Collector's Guide*, and *Gas Pump Collector's Guide*. Several changes have been made, though, for clarity, and to adapt to different types of collectibles. Each of the following types of collectibles has its own section: globes, signs, cans, maps, toys, and trinkets (certain items will require specific descriptive listings).

Descriptive Text

For all the collectibles covered in this book, several common features are used in descriptive text. They are as follows:

- *Flying Horse*: This always refers to the image of the red Pegasus that has been used in various forms for most of this century to identify Socony, and later Mobil, products.
- *Gargoyle*: Another trademark taken from mythology that was originally developed by Vacuum Oil Company for lubricants. The image usually appeared in red.
- *Socony Logo*: Always refers to the Socony "SONY & shield" logo, referred to in the following descriptions as a blue circle with a large white/red outlined five-point shield positioned to the circle's lower edge. A red line crosses the shield about one–third of the way down, with "SOCONY" in red above the line and "MOTOR GASOLINE" in red below the line. Small blue type reading "STANDARD OIL CO. OF NEW YORK" runs around the bottom edge of the shield. A distorted white "S" and "O" are in the blue area above the shield; an elongated "N" is to the left; and an elongated "Y" is to the right of the shield. Refer to this description from the text.
- *Mobilgas shield*: Refers to any one of the numerous five–pointed shields displaying the large red flying horse at the top. These logos—and there are numerous variations—were used from the early 1930s until the introduction of the "flat" shield in the 1950s.
- *Mobil Flat shield*: Refers to the logo that was first introduced in 1955 and came into common use in 1958. It was the first to feature the word "Mobil" alone on the emblem. The upper border is blue, and the lower border is formed by a red "chevron," notched in the center for a small version of the flying horse.
- *Quotation Marks*: Words within quotes indicate type as it appeared on the item. For example, "SOCONY" in a description means the word *SOCONY* appears in uppercase letters on the item.
- *Slash Marks*: The word or phrase preceding the slash is displayed above the word or phrase following the slash on whatever object is being described. For example, a sign bearing the description "GARGOYLE MOBILOIL/ MOBILGAS" has the phrase "GARGOYLE MOBIL-OIL" appearing above the word "MOBILGAS."

chapter one ....

Overview of the Petroleum Collectibles Hobby

*t*housands of people worldwide are involved in the petroleum collectibles hobby. Beginning in the 1940s people began accumulating paper items, gas pump globes, and early gas pumps on a very limited basis. It was only a very small number, too—fewer than 10 collectors were active in this era.

In the 1960s antique car enthusiasts began to seek out interesting service station items to accent their car collections, and several began to actively build their collections of globes and gas pumps. The 1970s saw the first national-level interest in the hobby, including the introduction of reproduction items to restore gas pumps. By the late 1970s several books were available on the hobby and the history of the petroleum marketing industry. The early 1980s saw the beginning of several regularly published periodicals dealing with petroleum collectibles, and by the mid-1980s more books were published and the first of the now-numerous regional swap meets was held.

The hobby exploded about 1989, with hundreds of new collectors joining in the fun every year. Most areas of the country were within a day's drive of some regional annual event. In 1990 the co-authors of this book teamed up to produce the first in a series of books designed specifically for today's collector of petroleum memorabilia. This book is number nine in a series that now includes plans for several others.

Of interest to our readers is the fact that the authors also offer the only complete monthly periodical serving the hobby, *Petroleum Collectibles Monthly*. When your copy arrives each month, you will find it filled with information on new discoveries, reproduction item alerts, events and auction coverage, a show schedule, a list of displays across the country that are open to the public as well as other places to visit, plus the largest

This array of Mobil collectibles offers something for everyone, including oil cans, signs, and toys.

Many single brand collectors create elaborate displays of collectibles featuring their particular brand. Often these displays take the form of a re-created service station. *Dave Mercer collection, PCM archives*

classified ad marketplace serving the hobby. For further information on the hobby, on books available, or to subscribe to *Petroleum Collectibles Monthly*, contact the authors at:

Petroleum Collectibles Monthly
P.O. Box 556
La Grange, OH 44050-0556
Phone: 440/355-6608
FAX: 440/355-4955

All of the authors' other books are also available through *Petroleum Collectibles Monthly*, including the self-published *Guide To Gasoline Logos*, a complete look at marketing symbols along with a system of dating virtually all petroleum collectibles. Contact *PCM* today for more information. In addition, author Scott Benjamin operates one of the largest sources of all original

9

In any collector display that is viewed by the passing public, protection from the elements and from vandalism is important. Rare original signage is placed high on the building, while pumps in weatherproof primer are topped by reproduction globes. *Dave Mercer collection, PCM archives*

petroleum collectibles. His business is called simply Oil Company Collectibles, and it can be reached at the same address and phone numbers listed above.

Collector Information and Collectible Background

As a service to readers of this book, we wish to make the following comments about the various types of petroleum collectibles and their relative interest among participants in the hobby today. They are listed in order of popularity.

Signs

Signs are considered the most popular petroleum collectible item today. The earliest signs were lithographed tin, and by 1920 porcelain began to see extensive use in the petroleum industry. Plastics, which were introduced to the industry in 1947 and appeared in common use after 1960, are much less collectible than the earlier tin and porcelain items. Neon was never extensively used in the gasoline industry, but collectors have recently taken interest in the few neon signs available.

Sign prices range from a mere $25 for a recent plastic item to more than $10,000 for the most decorative and artistic porcelain signs available. Many reproductions are available, so be careful and know what you are buying.

Mobil signs with unusual graphics are among the most desirable, and at the other end of the spectrum, the Mobil gas pump signs are perhaps the most commonly found petroleum sign of any kind. Signs were the primary subject of our earlier book, *Oil Company Signs: A Collector's Guide*, published by Motorbooks International in 1996.

Globes

Second only to signs in popularity are gas pump globes. From the earliest one-piece etched milk glass domes to the plastic-bodied globes still used by several companies today, each and every gas pump globe is highly collectible.

Globes evolved from the early one-piece glass globes into metal-band bodies with glass lenses, then into glass bodies with removable lenses, and finally into the plastic bodies formed in halves and sandwiched around lenses.

Generally, the more graphic the globe, the more desirable it is. Prices range from around $100 for plain plastic globes to more than $15,000 for the most unique globes available.

Mobil globes are among the most popular, and globes from Mobil affiliate Gilmore are among the highest-priced globes available. Many reproductions are available, so be careful and know what you are buying. Globes were the primary subject of our earlier book, *Gas Pump Globes*, released by Motorbooks International in 1994.

Despite the need for security, details are important in collector displays. Note the island light, water, and oil cans on the recreated pump island. *Dave Mercer collection, PCM archives*

Cans

Motor oil cans and other product containers first became popular among collectors in the late 1980s. Today the common quart can, used from the early 1930s until the mid-1980s, is the most popular format, but five-quart cans and handy oilers are also very popular.

As with signs and globes, the more graphic the can, the more desirable it is. Cans can be found in prices ranging from less than $5 for composite cans with plain graphics to nearly $2,000 for the most graphically appealing steel cans. Several reproductions are available, so be careful and know what you are buying. No definitive work on cans has yet been completed.

Pumps

The first surge in interest in petroleum collectibles focused on gas pumps in the 1960s. Visible pumps were most desirable then, although in recent years visibles and previsibles have taken a back seat to ornate clock-face and other mechanically intricate and decorative gas pumps. Mechanical calculating pumps, particularly with art deco designs, are very popular as well.

All pumps manufactured up until the "chrome" era of the 1960s are collectible. Globes were the primary subject of our earlier book, *Gas Pump Collector's Guide*, released by Motorbooks International in 1994.

Toys

Toys are relatively new as petroleum collectibles. Gasoline-related toys have been manufactured since the 1920s, and accurately detailed brand-specific toys have been offered since the 1930s. Some toys can be considered promotionals, while others were simply children's toys available to anyone (not just paying customers).

Mobil was one of the first companies to regularly allow the use of its image in normal stock, nonpromotional toys, and the company continues to do so today.

Prices range from the $20 range for new toys to well over $1,000 for toys made as recently as 15 years ago.

Maps and Paper Items

Many collectors started their collections as children collecting road maps. Free road maps were perhaps the most widespread oil company promotion of all time, with millions of maps being given away from 1914 to the present. Most companies, however, including Mobil, abandoned the practice in the 1970s.

All maps are considered collectible. Mobil maps are not as graphically appealing as those of some other brands, and as a result are not very valuable. While maps in general range in price from $1 to about $75, most Mobil maps fall into the $1 to $5 range.

Internal Corporate Items

Internal corporate items have recently grown in interest to collectors. Employee pins and badges, award items, and trinkets, many of which fall into the "smalls" or "trinkets" category, are addressed below.

Collectors are also interested in corporate publications, and their price ranges depend on the type of item involved. Many items are hard to find, since they were never mass-produced nor intended for use by the general public.

Trinkets

Advertising novelties are among the fastest growing categories of interest of all petroleum collectibles. Salt and pepper shaker sets, oil can banks, radios, and thousands more items are available. Virtually anything bearing an oil company logo is collectible.

Categories include items supplied by the oil companies themselves, items sanctioned by the oil companies and personalized by the local distributor or dealer, and items supplied by advertising companies directly to distributors and dealers. Price ranges vary greatly, and prices are rising.

History of the Mobil Oil Corporation

*t*he Standard Oil Company of New York, better known by its cable address acronym "SOCONY," was created in 1882 as the administrative division of the Standard Oil Trust, maintaining the various financial and office functions for the entire operation.

In the 1890s Socony ventured into refining and marketing, primarily for export. Soon Socony kerosene was known throughout Asia, and Socony developed an inexpensive lamp for its use, bringing modern illumination to the Orient. With the breakup of the Standard Oil Trust, Socony was left without crude reserves of any kind, and was forced to buy on the open market, primarily from Standard siblings The Ohio, Waters-Pierce, and South Penn. Socony had emerged from the breakup of Standard Oil in much the same situation that Standard of New Jersey was in: Standard had functioned well as a very complex industrial machine, each operation complementing the others well. Independently, though, the companies did not fare so well, as Socony's actions evidenced. With an extensive marketing network already in place, both in the Northeastern United States and in Asia, the company had little choice but to seek out the crude to refine and sell.

A Presence in the Northeast

Socony began branded gasoline marketing in New York and New England in 1915, a natural extension of

What more can be said of this sign? The flying red horse is one of the most recognized trademarks of this century. Mobil stations of all kinds displayed, in every manner possible, die-cut horses made of tin, porcelain, neon, plastic, and other materials. This example is one of the most popular for collectors, a "cookie cutter" horse, so called because it is die-cut and embossed in the shape and texture of the horse. *Dave Mercer collection, PCM archives*

the bulk facilities already in place. Prior to this time, some gasoline marketing had been attempted through regional jobbers, but lacking consistent supply, an extensive jobber network was not feasible. Instead, the company solicited independent dealers, and soon the Socony shield logo was known in every village and town in the territory.

To assure having a constant supply of crude oil to refine and sell, Socony purchased a minority interest in Dallas, Texas-based Magnolia Petroleum. Magnolia, primarily a production company, was a well-endowed crude oil supplier, having developed the Corsicana, Texas, oil fields. Magnolia had been founded in Corsicana in 1894, and by the time Socony purchased a minority interest in 1918, Magnolia was already a fully integrated oil company. The Socony-Magnolia merger was very successful, giving Socony access to crude and Magnolia sources of refined products to sell. Seven years later Socony acquired the balance of Magnolia, making it a wholly owned subsidiary.

The Socony-Magnolia merger was so successful that in 1926 Socony went looking for potential partners in a West Coast venture, eventually choosing General Petroleum. General, founded in 1910, was a pioneer company in the California oil fields. It had developed a refinery at Vernon, California, and was involved in marketing refined products all along the Pacific Coast in North and South America. In a sense, Socony was merging with operations somewhat more self-sufficient than its own, giving the new entities access to capital for expansion.

Socony was no doubt studying the map, particularly the marketing territories map, when negotiating mergers. Next in line came White Eagle Oil and Refining, based in Kansas City, Missouri. White Eagle was founded in 1916 as a production company, and it operated three strategically located refineries ideally suited to supply refined products to a network of bulk plants and filling stations all across the Midwest.

Socony purchased White Eagle in 1930. While crude production and refining capacity were of utmost importance to Socony, these three mergers had significantly increased Socony affiliated gasoline marketing, essentially from coast to coast. The various entities retained their identities, both in operation as subsidiary companies, and at the gas pump, where Socony, Magnolia, General, and White Eagle trademarks were all still proudly displayed. Despite this success, Socony's next merger would prove to be the most significant.

Vacuum: A Significant Acquisition

Vacuum Oil Works was founded in 1866 in Rochester, New York, as a lubricants refiner. Its earliest products, kerosene and various lubricants, were distilled by a special process using a vacuum, hence the company's unusual name. By 1879, when Standard purchased Vacuum Oil, Vacuum was the largest producer of branded lubricants in the world. In the Standard era, Vacuum's oils were marketed under the "Gargoyle" brand name, and among its most famous products was a superior oil for the new gasoline engines coming into everyday use. The new product, introduced about 1904, was called "Gargoyle Mobiloil."

Standard's status as a truly integrated operation was greatly enhanced by the Gargoyle products, and virtually every one of the Standard marketing divisions sold Gargoyle oils. When Standard was broken up in 1911, Vacuum emerged in the somewhat unusual position of having an excellent product manufactured through excellent facilities, but with virtually no sales department through which to market it.

While most of the Standard siblings scrambled for crude, Vacuum scrambled to get marketing exposure. Fortunately, since most of the former siblings were without a premier line of lubricants, they continued to purchase Vacuum's products, marketing them all over the world. As a marketing department was developed, many independent gasoline marketers, garages, and other oil companies were signed on to the Mobiloil program. Gargoyle Mobiloil signs were probably among the most common sights along the nation's roadsides during the 1911 to 1930 era.

The "Mobilgas" Name Expands

By the middle 1920s Vacuum had expanded into gasoline marketing in Ohio, Pennsylvania, and the Chicago area under the "Mobilgas" brand name. In this era the Mobilgas brand was always closely identified with the corporate name "Vacuum Oil."

In 1929 Vacuum Oil purchased St. Louis-based Lubrite Refining Company, a company that was primarily a lubricants refiner, but operated gasoline stations in Missouri, Iowa, Illinois, and Indiana. Use of the Lubrite name continued, although the gasoline sold carried the Mobilgas brand, almost as if it were a franchise. Vacuum Oil's Mobilgas was now available from the Atlantic Coast all the way to Iowa. Not content to rest with the success of this expansion, Vacuum began negotiations to purchase an even larger marketer.

Milwaukee-based Wadhams Oil Company was founded in the 1870s as a specialty lubricants marketer, and by 1915 had began building up a network of gasoline stations throughout Wisconsin and Minnesota, and in the Chicago area. A company known for flamboyant marketing, Wadhams constructed stations resembling Chinese pagodas, with various sizes designed for the size of the particular local population.

In 1929 Wadhams purchased its largest independent competitor, Milwaukee neighbor Bartles McGuire Oil Company. With the addition of the former Bartles "Bonded" stations, Wadhams became a leading marketer in Wisconsin, and an early proponent of the "Red Hat" association, the Independent Oil Men of America (IOMA). Vacuum Oil landed a big one with the 1930 purchase of Wadhams. Wadhams continued to operate as a semi-independent subsidiary, although Mobilgas branding began to appear alongside the Wadhams brand.

Expanding Even Further

To further solidify its position in America's industrial Upper Midwest, Vacuum Oil went shopping again, this time in Detroit. In 1930 Vacuum purchased Detroit-based White Star Refining Company, adding more than 1,500 stations to the Vacuum Oil "Mobilgas" marketing map in Ohio, Indiana, and Michigan. White Star was a well-established brand, and again, the Mobilgas name was added alongside White Star, almost as if Mobilgas were a franchise product.

As 1931 dawned, both Socony and Vacuum were independently successful Standard siblings, having overcome early obstacles to become two of America's most successful oil companies. Socony was a motor fuels marketer, while Vacuum was a lubricants manufacturer that just happened to have a solid position in gasoline marketing using a trademark tied to its successful lubricants line. Court approval was necessary for the companies to join, and in 1931 these two successful siblings reunited to form Socony-Vacuum Oil Company.

Since both Socony and Vacuum were the products of many mergers and acquisitions, no uniform image existed from region to region within the company. The 1931 merger only added to this somewhat confused marketplace presence. Vacuum had used the "Mobilgas" brand almost as if it were a franchise or a licensed product such as "Ethyl." Socony had never even standardized this much, and its affiliate stations retained their original brands and images. With the merger, however, the new entity became determined to take advantage of its nationwide presence with a single national identity.

Developing an Identity

Vacuum's Mobilgas brand name was the best known of all of the brand names in use, primarily because of its ties to Mobiloil. Socony had several foreign subsidiaries using a Pegasus design to symbolize speed and power, attributes certainly desirable to petroleum products. By 1934 it was decided to tie the Mobilgas brand to the Socony Pegasus for a unified national image. Those affiliates wishing to retain some identity of their own could continue to display the subsidiary name in a secondary position across the bottom of the shield logo chosen, a design adapted from that used by Socony from its beginnings in gasoline.

Soon, "Mobilgas-Wadhams" or "Mobilgas-White Star" (logo only) shields appeared as station identifications throughout the respective territories. Regional gasoline brand names were abandoned in 1934 in favor of Mobilgas (regular) and Mobilgas Ethyl (premium), which was renamed Mobilgas Special in 1936.

Despite this unity, merger fever had not left the new company. The search continued for marketing companies that would solidify Socony's position in those areas where the company already had supply and distribution facilities. To this end, in 1934 the newly united Socony-Vacuum purchased two regional marketers, Independent Oil of Altoona, Pennsylvania, and Metro Oil of Jamestown, New York. Metro had long been affiliated with Socony, having been an early wholesale distributor of Socony products. The Metro name was preserved as Socony-Vacuum's brand name for motor grade gasoline as late as 1955.

Further expansion on the West Coast was accomplished with the 1940 purchase of controlling interest in California's most image-conscious marketer, Gilmore Oil Company. Gilmore was nothing short of a flamboyant marketing company, an early sponsor of automobile racing, and an excellent addition, through the General Petroleum subsidiary, to Mobilgas marketing. World War II intervened before Gilmore stations could be completely reimaged, but by the end of 1945 the "Red Lion" had jumped off into the western sunset, chased away by Socony-Vacuum's "Flying Red Horse."

Post–War Brand Awareness Soars

The end of World War II marked the beginning of the modern era of Socony-Vacuum's marketing, as the various regional images were eliminated, and Mobilgas and Mobiloil became two of America's most recognized trademarks. The Mobilgas shield appeared in all states across the country except those in the Deep South. Always on the leading edge of marketing images, the famed Mobil flying horse leapt in porcelain and neon across station facades, on rooftops, on signs, and pumps. With the advent of plastic signage, Mobil became the first company to avail itself of 1950s image studies, and it recreated its logo to better accommodate the new material. The new elongated shield was introduced in 1955, gradually replacing the classic shield by 1958, although the Mobilgas and Mobilgas Special gasoline brands remained in use until 1962, when they were replaced with Mobil Regular and Mobil Premium, using the new logo in advertising. Stations were reimaged as well, with blue becoming a more dominant color in station design.

In the early 1960s Mobil became a participant in the Keep America Beautiful campaign, designing a station that could be built in harmony with surroundings in suburban neighborhoods. Known as the "Pegasus," the station prototype was unveiled in 1964. Featuring round pump island canopies standing like mushrooms over polished stainless steel cylindrical pumps, the Pegasus was a significant departure from Mobil station designs in use up until that time. Natural color brick and wood, even stone, were selected as building materials. Along with the Shell "rancher," Mobil's new design led the way in the trend for beautification of the service station in the 1960s.

Socony Mobil Oil Company, the corporate name adopted in 1955, became simply Mobil Oil Company in 1966. With the new name a new logo was introduced, with Mobil lettering in blue except for the "o" in red. Design awards were again bestowed on Mobil, as the new logos went up as station signage at Pegasus-style stations nationwide. The famed flying horse was relocated to a position of lesser prominence, appearing on illuminated discs on station building signage. With the reimaging, the flying horse appeared on a white disc wherever used, whether on tank trucks or in print. Gray became a more prominent color in the marketing image as well, a trend all of Mobil's competitors would follow more than 20 years later.

The gas shortage years of the 1970s saw Mobil diversify with the purchase of "Marcor," parent organization of Montgomery Ward and Container Corporation of America. Suddenly an oil company was a major retailer as well. Government attacks on the petroleum industry were countered by Mobil advertising, a practice the company maintains to the present.

Mobil began conversion of some unprofitable company-owned locations in the late 1970s into self-serve, convenience store "Reelo" and "Sello" stations. The experiment with convenience stores with its secondary brands opened the doors to branded Mobil involvement. Today more than 2,000 of Mobil's 7,000-plus stations are company direct-operated convenience stores. Many of the other 5,000 or so Mobil outlets are jobber-operated convenience stores as well. Mobil, always a lubricants leader, was a pioneer in this field also, with "Mobil 1" being the first widely marketed synthetic motor oil when it was introduced in 1975.

Mobil today ranks second in assets behind Exxon, with more than $40 billion. Mobil sold the Marcor interests in the 1980s to concentrate on its core businesses in energy production. Mobil's Flying Red Horse is certainly one of the world's most widely recognized trademarks, identifying Mobil products worldwide.

This classic example of the 1964 Mobil "Pegasus" station design is still functioning in Mocksville, North Carolina, where it was built in 1968 when Interstate 40 was extended through the area. *PCM archives*

This roadside grocery and tavern was selling Mobilgas products in upstate New York in the 1930s. *Courtesy of Mike Thibaut, PCM archives*

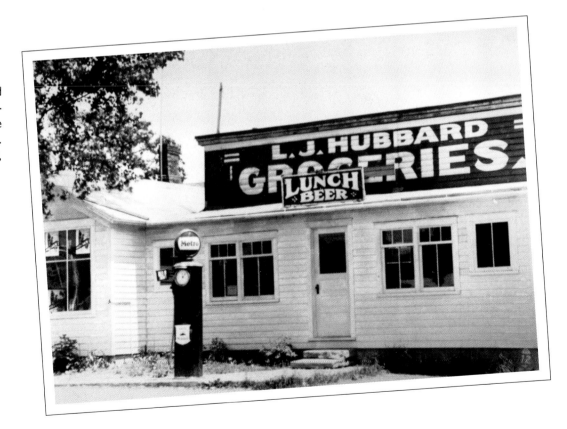

Mobil Service Station Design

*t*he first station design to give Mobil a unified look was the "drum" station, which was developed by architect Frederick Frost in 1940 from an adaptation of earlier designs by industrial designer Norman Bel Geddes. The station features a rectangular footprint, with any number of service bays possible and optional left- and right-hand layouts. The most striking feature of these stations is the front corner of the office area of the station, which is rounded and projects above the rest of the roofline. This corner parapet is symbolic of Mobil's longtime symbol, the oil drum.

The station is finished in white porcelain panels, with a red band around the base, and parallel red bands set just above the window line and just below the roofline, forming a red outlined white panel across the top of the station. The flying red horse is featured prominently on this panel, centered at the extent of the radius of the drum. Dark blue porcelain lettering reading "Mobilgas," "Mobiloil," and "Mobil-ubrication" is positioned accordingly along the panel as well. Surviving examples are quite rare.

Many roadside motor courts of the 1930s and '40s sold gasoline in addition to renting rooms or cabins. This station was located along Highway 10 in Columbus, Montana. *Courtesy of Bob Mewes, PCM archives*

White and Red Porcelain Station

Around 1950, Mobil designers modified the earlier drum station, eliminating the rounded office corner area but maintaining the color scheme. Most noticeable with this design is the three-dimensional porcelain flying horse logo that projects above the roofline positioned just off the centerline of the station façade, usually just above the office door. There were thousands of these stations built over an approximate 15-year time span and a few still remain in use today.

Light Blue Porcelain Façade

In 1963 Mobil modified the earlier station design, replacing the white façade offset by red stripes with a more subdued light blue porcelain façade. Station lettering was modified as well, with the office area simply identified by the word "Mobil" in lettering identical to that found on the new flat shield sign.

This Ford garage in Mott, North Dakota, was selling White Eagle gasoline in 1933. Within several years the eagles would be gone and the Mobil image would be in place. *Courtesy of Bob Mewes, PCM archives*

Service bays were identified by lettering of the same style reading simply "Mobil Service." The flying red horse projecting above the roofline remained a prominent feature as in the earlier stations. Surviving examples of this design are much rarer, since these stations were built in much smaller numbers over several years only.

Pegasus

In 1964 Mobil Oil commissioned architect Elliot Noyes to develop a complete reimaging for Mobil stations using the new age image designs developed by industrial designers Chermayeff and Geismar Associates. The result would eventually be applied to more than 15,000 Mobil stations nationwide.

Working from the 1940 image of the oil drum, a complete series of station features were developed using circular designs. Most notable were the gas pumps, typical Gilbarco "Trimline" pumps with modified cabinetry of brushed stainless steel, shaped just like an oil drum. The pump was lighted with a flat, circular, white plastic fixture covering its entire top.

The circular theme carried over to the canopies as well, as they were circular, perhaps 20 feet in diameter, and supported by a single center pole. The station design itself was rather stark in nature, with large glass ex-panses broken up by opaque blue panels, all set in brick primary walls.

The flying red horse, now removed from the station sign with the introduction of the "red O" image, is featured prominently on white illuminated circular panels mounted along the horizontal centerline of one of the brick walls. A narrow white band along the parapet allowed for the installation of plastic lettering reading "Mobil Service." Hundreds of these stations survive intact, and more still in various conversions to convenience stores.

Mobil Affiliates

We cannot discuss Mobilgas architecture without at least a mention of the beautiful Wadhams "Pagoda" stations built by Mobil affiliate Wadhams throughout Wisconsin in the 1920s. In an effort to attract attention, Wadhams constructed numerous stations in the design of a Chinese pagoda temple.

An elaborate roofline and detailing were key elements. After Wadhams was fully merged into Socony-Vacuum, the Mobilgas image was added to the pagoda stations, and some really unusual examples exist today sporting the gray and white 1966 image with the illuminated disc and flying red horse. Watch for these throughout Wisconsin.

Classic Mobilgas architecture survives along Gratiot Avenue between Detroit and Mount Clemens, Michigan. This service station was built in 1946 and survives relatively intact today. The station is an excellent example of the Frederick Frost architectural design adopted by Mobil in 1940. Note the adjacent store to the left of the station that mimics the architectural design. *Wayne Henderson photo, PCM archives*

Lyon's Oil Company operated this classic Mobilgas station in Wathena, Kansas, in the 1960s. Note that one service bay has been closed in, for an office for the oil company. *PCM Archives*

A more recent photo showing the Mobil image of the 1950s was captured in this 1985 photo by author Wayne Henderson. This was the flagship station for Goochland, Virginia–based Marsh Oil Company. *Wayne Henderson photo, PCM archives*

A rare surviving example of the short-lived 1960s design that sported a light blue upper facade was captured in this 1987 photo in Upper Sandusky, Ohio. *Wayne Henderson photo, PCM archives*

Some of our favorite station photos involve a juxtaposing of images. Here the Frederick Frost 1940 "drum" station displays the color scheme adopted in 1966 for those stations that were not rebuilt into the "Pegasus" design. This station was discovered in Port Huron, Michigan, in 1987. *Wayne Henderson photo, PCM archives*

Round pumps, round canopies, all a continuation of the drum image. This Mocksville, North Carolina, station was photographed in 1989. *Wayne Henderson photo, PCM archives*

The central theme of the "Pegasus" station is this disc. With the 1964 introduction of the design, the flying red horse was added to a white circular sign that became the central element of station architecture. Note that the direction the horse is jumping changed with this image, although some earlier examples of the horse facing right are known in special applications. *Wayne Henderson photo, PCM archives*

The "red O" Mobil sign, officially adopted in 1964 and introduced into common use in 1966, was one of the first gasoline trademarks to adopt a European look. This sign serves as primary identification at thousands of stations worldwide, although this particular example is found on Outer Drive in Dearborn, Michigan. *Wayne Henderson photo, PCM archives*

Modern Mobil stations feature clean imaging. Many traditional stations have been converted to convenience stores in recent years, although this station on U.S. 58 in Courtland, Virginia, was actually built as a convenience store. It is owned and operated by Mobil distributor S. W. Rawls of Franklin, Virginia. *Wayne Henderson photo, PCM archives*

Here the Mobilgas image is enhanced with the inclusion of a neon Mobilgas shield. This station, originally a White Rose outlet, was operating in Memphis about 1950. *Chip Flohe*

Perhaps the car speeding through this photo is running on Mobil Premium from the 1960s Mobil station in Memphis. *Chip Flohe*

Commonplace today, but quite rare for this era, is this Memphis Mobilgas station that included a car wash. Note the revolving neon flying horse at curbside. *Chip Flohe*

Home and auto stores often sold gasoline, as did this Memphis tire dealer. This photo was taken about 1950 in Memphis, Tennessee. *Chip Flohe*

The Mobilgas image at its best! A huge, double-faced porcelain Mobilgas shield and smaller Mobiloil curb sign identify this station in Memphis about 1956. *Chip Flohe*

Open-air service areas and free-hanging canopies were features of many West Coast stations, including the Gilmore station from the mid-1930s. *Ron Johnson photo, PCM archives*

A rooftop red lion stands guard atop this California Gilmore station in 1936. *Ron Johnson photo, PCM archives*

This mini-station in California was dispensing Gilmore products during the middle 1930s. Often commercial garages would add these stations in the driveway area for an added profit center. *Ron Johnson photo, PCM archives*

Here we see a more conventional single-bay Gilmore station that advertises the Gilmore "Chek-Chart" lubrication service. *Ron Johnson photo, PCM archives*

chapter four ....

Mobil Globes

ocony was one of the first gasoline marketers to attempt to develop a consistent image throughout its marketing territory. One of the tools employed to accomplish this was the branded pump top globes on virtually every gas pump that dispensed Socony products. In parallel with this, Vacuum Oil, in an attempt to promote its Mobiloil products, was providing retailers with outdoor island cabinets to store Mobiloil lubricants.

Prominently displayed atop each cabinet was an oval light-up globe displaying Vacuum's "Gargoyle" and brand-name "Mobiloil." Other marketers that would eventually affiliate with Socony and Vacuum or the combined operation began using branded globes in the late 1910s. Indeed, one of the most majestic of all globes was the cast white eagle, representing, of course, White Eagle products sold throughout the central states.

Mobil was an international marketer, and this one-piece glass globe with the baked-on image of the 1966 logo was used in Europe in the late 1960s. *Dave Mercer collection, PCM archives*

Left
For the Mobil globe collector, there are hundreds of globes to select from. This oval globe dates from the 1920s and early 1930s. Mobil was an international marketer, and this one-piece glass globe with the baked-on image of the 1966 logo was used in Europe in the late 1960s. *Dave Mercer collection, PCM archives*

Typical of the early 1960s image is this Mobilfuel Diesel globe used from 1962 through 1966. It matches the pump sign of the same era. *Dave Mercer collection, PCM archives*

Each globe listing in this chapter contains the following:

Globe Title, Rarity Code, Years Used, Type of Globe, Body Type, Body Color (metal body only), Price Range, and Descriptive Text. These can be interpreted as follows:

Globe Title

This is simply the name commonly used by collectors to refer to the globe.

Rarity Code

A numerical code system can be interpreted as follows:

(1): A very common globe, one that's readily available in collector circles.
(2): A common globe; fairly readily available among collectors.
(3): Available. These globes, though available, are a little more scarce.
(4): Rare—few are known to exist. They are around but are much harder to find.
(5): Extremely rare—fewer than 10 are known to exist; rarely found or offered for sale.
(6): Unique—one of a kind. If a (6) appears, there is only one such globe known to exist. If another (6) is found, that first globe then becomes a (5).

(7): Known only in old photographs. If a (7) appears, then as of this writing one does not exist! Once discovered, a (7) will then become a (6)!
(8): An unfortunate category. If an (8) appears, then the only known example of this globe was broken and discarded! This has happened to a few globes, and we needed a special category for it. If another (8) is found, then the first globe will become a (6). Let's hope that happens.
(9): Strong evidence suggests this globe exists. If a globe appears as a (9), then we have official drawings made by a company, a known mate to that globe—regular/ethyl—or a sketch on a road map or another source. During the writing of this book many (9)s became (6)s or were discovered in a collection. You may have such a globe. If so, let us know and when this book is updated we will categorize it properly.

These additional categories [(8) and (9)] will immediately tell the rarity of an item. It will sort out things like why a Wadhams Mobilgas three–piece glass globe with the small shield at the top is never seen—because it is a (7).

Years Used

This refers to the number of years that this item would have been placed in service in a new installation. In practice, many items remained in use long after they had been officially replaced.

Type of Globe

The globe's body style and size. Abbreviations can be interpreted as follows:
• OPE—One-piece etched globe.
• OPB—One-piece globe with a baked enamel finish.
• OPC—One-piece cast globe with raised or recessed details.
• CAPCO—Plastic-body globe manufactured by Cincinnati Advertising Products Company consisting of two plastic body halves assembled around glass (or rarely, plastic) lenses.

Body Type

For one-piece globes:
N = narrow one-piece body;
RW = rounded wide one-piece body;
W = wide one-piece body;
OPB = one-piece baked;
OPE = one-piece etched;
OPC = one-piece cast;
OPP = one-piece with painted (not baked on) details.
For three-piece glass globes:
N = narrow glass body;
W = wide glass body.
For metal globes:
L or LP = low-profile metal body;

H or HP = high-profile metal body. If the original color for the metal body is known, it will be listed as "H red" or "L blue," etc.

Body Color

These listings simply show the color that a metal body was painted as part of the original color scheme. You may find that as globes have been in the hands of collectors, bodies are painted to please the owners and may not match the original company color schemes. Use your own judgment as to whether you display them in their original colors or one more pleasing. Where no listing appears, we are uncertain of the original color scheme.

Price Range

The prices in this book are listed as a range—from wholesale to retail. Ranges are left between the two prices to allow for variations in condition, negotiation, etc. A price of $1,500 to $2,200 simply means that $1,500 is a wholesale value and $2,200 is the top retail value. Both are considered good deals within their respective definitions.

Socony Note

The Socony "SONY & shield" logo referred to in the following descriptions is a blue circle with a large white/red outlined five-point shield positioned at the lower edge of the circle. A red line crosses the shield about one–third of the way down with red "SOCONY" above the line and red "MOTOR GASOLINE" below the line. There is a small blue "STANDARD OIL CO. OF NEW YORK" around the bottom edge of the shield, a distorted white "S" and "O" in the blue area above the shield, and an elongated "N" to the left and "Y" to the right of shield. Refer to this description from the globe text below.

Mobil Globes Listings

Socony (sphere)
(7) 1915–1918 OPE   No Listing
White spherical globe with blue "SOCONY" across globe face.

Socony Motor Gasoline
(5) 1915–1920 OPE   W $2,500–3,800
White globe with blue/white outlined SONY & shield logo as described above on globe face. Often found with large metal protective cover that encircles globe and base.

Socony Motor Gasoline (milk glass lens)
(4) 1915–1926 16.5" Metal   HP Red $1,200–1,800
Socony Motor Gasoline (milk glass lens)
(4) 1915–1926 15" Metal   HP Red $1,200–1,800
Socony Motor Gasoline (milk glass lens)
(5) 1915–1926 14" Metal   HP Red $1,700–2,200
Socony Motor Gasoline (milk glass lens)
(5) 1915–1926 13.675" Metal HP Red $1,800–2,400

Typical of the early 1960s image is this Mobil Premium globe used from 1962 through 1966. It matches the pump sign of the same era. *Dave Mercer collection, PCM archives*

Milk glass globe face with white outline ring around SONY & shield logo as described earlier.

Socony Motor Gasoline
(6) 1915–1926 16.5" Metal   HP Red $1,800–2,400
Socony Motor Gasoline
(6) 1915–1926 15" Metal   HP Red $1,800–2,400
Globe has white outline ring around SONY & shield as described earlier.

Socony Motor Gasoline (flat porcelain lens)
(5) 1915–1926 15" Metal   HP Red $2,000–2,600
Socony Motor Gasoline (curved porcelain lens)
(6) 1915–1926 15" Metal   HP Red $2,000–2,600
Socony Motor Gasoline (porcelain lens)
(5) 1915–1926 14" Metal   HP Red $2,000–2,500
Socony Motor Gasoline (cast lens)
(6) 1915–1926 16.5" Metal   HP Red   No Listing
Socony Motor Gasoline (cast lens)
(5) 1915–1926 15" Metal   HP Red $2,000–2,600
White globe face with blue/white outlined SONY & shield logo as described above on globe face.

Socony
(3) 1926–1934 16.5" Metal   HP Red $300–550

Typical of the early 1960s image is this Mobil Regular globe used from 1962 through 1966. It matches the pump sign of the same era. *Dave Mercer collection, PCM archives*

Socony
(3) 1926–1934 15" Metal   HP Red $300–550
White globe face with red "SOCONY" with blue drop shadow across center.

Socony red lettering w/white lines
(3) 1926–1934 16.5" Metal   HP Red $300–550
Socony red lettering w/white lines
(3) 1926–1934 15" Metal   HP Red $300–550
White globe face with red "SOCONY" with blue drop shadow across center—red lettering with white lines.

Socony Special milk glass lens
(4) 1922–1926 16.5" Metal   HP Red $900–1,300
Socony Special milk glass lens
(5) 1922–1926 15" Metal   HP Red $900–1,400
White milk glass globe face with red "SOCONY" arched around top, "GASOLINE" around bottom with blue "SPECIAL" across center.

Socony Special (normal painted lens)
(6) 1922–1926 15" Metal   HP Red $700–1,000
White milk glass globe face with red "SOCONY" arched around top, "GASOLINE" around bottom with blue "SPECIAL" across center.

Socony Ethyl (EGC)
(3) 1926–1934 16.5" Metal   HP Red $325–575
Socony Ethyl (EGC)
(3) 1926–1934 15" Metal   HP Red $325–575
White globe face with red "SOCONY" with blue drop shadow across center. Black outlined white circle at top of globe face with small Ethyl (EGC) logo. Red "ETHYL" with blue drop shadow below "SOCONY."

Socony Ethyl (w/lines)
(3) 1926–1934 16.5" Metal   HP Red $325–575
Socony Ethyl (w/lines)
(3) 1926–1934 15" Metal   HP Red $325–575
White globe face with blue outline ring and red "SOCONY" with blue drop shadow across center. Black outlined white circle at top of globe face with small Ethyl (EGC) logo. Red "ETHYL" with blue drop shadow below "SOCONY." Blue line under "ETHYL."

Socony Aviation Gasoline
(6) 1920s   16.5" Metal   HP Red $1,600–2,200
White milk glass globe face with red "SOCONY" arched around top, "GASOLINE" around bottom, blue "AVIATION" across center.

Socony Motor Oils (small w/4" base)
(6) 1915–1920 OPE   N $1,300–1,800
Small one-piece globe with 4" base and blue "SOCONY" over "MOTOR OILS" on face.

Socony Motor Oils
(5) 1915–1920 OPE   RW $1,200–1750
Socony Motor Oils
(5) 1915–1920 OPB   W $1,000–1,400
One–piece globe with blue "SOCONY" over "MOTOR OILS" on face.

Socony Burning Oil
(4) 1934–1940 16.5" Metal   HP Red $1,250–1750
Socony Burning Oil
(4) 1934–1940 15" Metal   HP Red $1,250–1750
White globe face with small flying red horse at top. Blue "SOCONY BURNING OIL" on lower globe face.

Standard Kerosene
(4) 1934–1940 15" Metal   HP Red $750–1,000
White globe face with small red flying horse at top. Blue "STANDARD" over "KEROSENE" on lower globe face.

Magnolia Petroleum
Dallas, Texas

A Texas oil producer/refiner/marketer dating from 1911, Magnolia sold 45 percent interest to Socony in 1918. Socony completed the purchase in 1925. The Magnolia brand name was replaced by "MOBILGAS" about

1934, after the Socony-Vacuum merger. Magnolia remained a separate, named subsidiary, primarily involved in pipeline transportation, until 1960.

Magnolia Gasoline
(7) 1915–1920 OPE   No Listing
White globe with red "MAGNOLIA" arched around top, "GASOLINE" around bottom of globe face.

Magnolia Gasoline
(6) 1920–1922 16.5" Metal   HP Red   No Listing
White globe face with no outline ring. Black outlined red "MAGNOLIA" arched around top, "GASOLINE" around bottom with detailed brown and gold flower magnolia blossom in center.

Magnolia Gasoline w/seven-leaf flower
(4) 1920–1926 16.5" Metal   HP Red $1,700–2,200
White globe face with red outline ring. Blue outlined red "MAGNOLIA" arched around top, "GASOLINE" around bottom with detailed "SEVEN" green leaf/white flower magnolia blossom in center.

Magnolia Gasoline w/five-leaf flower
(5) 1920–1926 16.5" Metal   HP Red $1,700–2,200
White globe face with red outline ring. Blue outlined red "MAGNOLIA" arched around top, "GASOLINE" around bottom with detailed "FIVE" green leaf/white flower magnolia blossom in center.

Magnolia Maximum Mileage
(3) 1926–1934 16.5" Metal   HP Red $1,700–2,200
White globe face with blue outline ring. Blue outlined red "MAGNOLIA" arched around top, "GASOLINE" around bottom with small detailed green leaf/white flower magnolia blossom in center. Blue "MAXIMUM" to left of flower, "MILEAGE" to right.

Magnolia Anti–Knock
(5) 1922–1926 16.5" Metal   HP Red $1,600–2,100
White globe face with blue outline ring. Wide dark blue band across center with large white "ANTI-KNOCK" across center band. Red "MAGNOLIA" arched around top, "GASOLINE" around bottom with detailed flower above band on upper globe face.

Magnolia Ethyl (EGC)
(4) 1926–1934 16.5" Metal   HP Red $750–1,000
Blue outline ring around red globe face. White/blue outline around white center circle. White "MAGNOLIA" arched around top, "GASOLINE" around bottom with small Ethyl (EGC) logo in center.

One of the more unusual globes to display the Flying Horse is this Socony Burning Oil globe used on pumps dispensing heating oil in the Northeast in the 1930s. *Dave Mercer collection, PCM archives*

General Petroleum Corporation
Vernon, California

A pioneer California oil producer and refiner, General was founded in 1910. In 1926 Socony purchased General Petroleum and maintained the General brands until the end of World War II, gradually replacing them with Mobilgas. As with Magnolia, General remained a separate, named subsidiary until 1960.

General Petroleum Products
(5) 1920–1928 15" Metal   No Listing
Green globe face with black areas above and below center. White "GENERAL" on center section, with other smaller white lettering in black areas.

General Gasoline
(4) 1928–1934 15" Metal $700–1,000
White globe face with red line above and below center. Script blue "GENERAL" above blue "GASOLINE" between red lines.

General Violet Ray Gasoline
(5) 1928–1932 15" Metal $3,000–4,000
White globe face with large green diamond covering most

For many years the flying horse appeared on Mobilgas globes. This metal band globe was used on pumps beginning in some markets in 1932 and continuing as late as 1962. *Dave Mercer collection, PCM archives*

of globe face. White band across center of diamond with red outlined purple "VIOLET RAY" on band. White "GENERAL" and purple lightning bolt in upper area of green diamond. Red "ANTI–KNOCK" in lower area of green diamond above wide white band. Red "GASO-LINE" extending beyond edge of diamond on lower band.

General Ethyl
(5) 1926–1934 15" Metal $2,000–2,500
Red upper globe face with green lower face. Large red outlined white triangular shield covers most of globe face with red/white/green checkerboard pattern at top of shield, small Ethyl (EGC) logo on lower shield.

General Petroleum Ethyl Gasoline
(6) 1942   13.5" Glass   No Listing
White globe face with blue outline ring. Red "GENERAL" arched around top, "PETROLEUM" around bottom with small Ethyl (EGC) logo in center, and small blue "GASO-LINE" below logo.

White Eagle Oil and Refining
Kansas City, Missouri

This mid-continent producer/refiner/marketer had gas stations in 11 Midwestern states. Chief White Eagle was a leader of the Ponca Indians in Oklahoma. White Eagle was first used as a corporate name in 1916 when L. L. Marcell founded the White Eagle Petroleum Company. That same year the new company built a refinery at Augusta, Kansas, having a capacity of 2,000 barrels per day.

In 1919 the White Eagle Petroleum Company was reorganized and the name changed to the White Eagle Oil and Refining Company. This reorganization was in reality a merger of six independent oil companies, and within a few years the new company enjoyed second position in the distribution of petroleum products in the Midwest. A second refinery was built at Casper, Wyoming, and one was purchased at Fort Worth, Texas.

The poised White Eagle was adopted as an emblem because of its dignity and general significance, particularly in the company's territory, and because it was in keeping with the company name. As a service station identification, this emblem—the big iron eagle in front of the station and the illuminated glass eagles on the pumps—was very effective.

In January 1930, the White Eagle Oil and Refining Company was purchased by the Standard Oil Company of New York (Socony), and the name was changed to the White Eagle Oil Corporation. When Socony and Vacuum merged in 1931, White Eagle Oil Corporation became a subsidiary company. In 1935 the White Eagle Oil Corporation was dissolved and the operation became the White Eagle division of Socony-Vacuum Oil Company, Inc.

White Eagle Gasoline
(5) 1918–1920 OPE   W $7,500–10,000

Another unusual Socony globe is this Socony Kerosene on a metal band. *Dave Mercer collection, PCM archives*

White globe with black and white perched eagle in center of globe face. Red "WHITE EAGLE" arched around top, "GASOLINE" around bottom.

White Eagle Gasoline and Oils
(5) 1920–1925 15" Metal $1,700–2,200
White globe face with black octagon outline. Black outlined red circle in center of black/white outlined black band across center. White "WHITE EAGLE" in black band, white "GASOLINE" arched around top of red circle, "AND OILS" arched around bottom.

White Eagle blunt nose
(3) 1924–1932 Eagle $1,300–1,600
Cast white eagle with very little detail and blunt nose.

White Eagle slit throat
(3) 1924–1932 Eagle $1,300–1,600
Same as above with casting line around throat.

White Eagle pointed nose, some detail
(4) 1930–1932 Eagle $1,600–2,100
Cast white eagle with more feather detail and pointed nose.
White Eagle pointed nose, good detail
(4) 1932   Eagle $1,800–2,400
Cast white eagle with very good feather detail and pointed nose.

After the merger of Socony and Vacuum in 1932, Mobilgas became the brand name for the regular grade gasoline sold by most of the Socony-Vacuum affiliates. Mobilgas pumps displayed globes such as this, found here on a glass body, from 1932 until 1962. *Dave Mercer collection, PCM archives*

Vacuum Oil Company
Rochester, New York

Founded as a lubricants manufacturer in 1866, Vacuum had developed an extensive line of specialty lubricants when Standard Oil purchased the company in 1879. During the Standard era, Vacuum's lubricants, under the Gargoyle and later Gargoyle Mobiloil brands, were sold by the various Standard marketing firms. With the breakup of Standard in 1911, Vacuum was left to market its oils through independent channels worldwide. It became involved with gasoline marketing, under the "MOBILGAS" brand, and expanded the gasoline venture with the purchase of Lubrite Refining Co. of St. Louis, Missouri, in 1929.

The following year Vacuum purchased Wadhams Oil Corporation of Milwaukee and the Vacuum "MOBILGAS" name was added to Wadhams' extensive product line. In 1930 Vacuum purchased White Star Refining of Detroit and added more than 1,500 outlets for Mobilgas. In 1931 Socony and Vacuum merged to form Socony Vacuum Oil Company, and after a two–year reimaging

program, the Mobilgas brand name became the company's primary brand, although several of the regional marketers retained their own identities until after World War II.

Mobilgas (progressive red & white lines)
(4) 1928–1930 16.5" Metal HP Red $800–1,200
Mobilgas (progressive red & white lines)
(4) 1928–1930 15" Metal HP Red $800–1,200
Mobilgas (progressive red & white lines)
(6) 1928–1930 13.5" Glass W No Listing
Red globe face with series of increasing-width white horizontal lines above and below white center band. Black "MOBILGAS" across white center band.

Mobilgas (milk glass)
(6) 1928–1930 15" Metal HP Red No Listing
Milk glass red globe face with series of increasing-width white horizontal lines above and below white center band. Black "MOBILGAS" across white center band.

Mobilgas (progressive red & white lines & horse)
(6) 1931–1934 15" Metal HP Red No Listing
Red globe face with series of increasing-width white horizontal lines above and below white center band. Black "MOBILGAS" across white center band. Small red Pegasus logo at top of globe face, possibly a decal.

Mobilgas—blue lettering w/red line
(2) 1932–1933 16.5" Metal L/H Red $300–550
Mobilgas—blue lettering w/red line
(2) 1932–1933 15" Metal L/H Red $300–550
Mobilgas—blue lettering w/red line
(3) 1932–1933 13.5" Glass W $250–375
White globe face with thin red line positioned above and below center, forming a white band across the center of globe face. Dark blue "MOBILGAS" in center band.

Mobilgas—(cast face) blue lettering w/red line
(6) 1932–1933 15" Metal L/H Red No Listing
Cast face with white globe face with thin red line positioned above and below center, forming a white band across the center of globe face. Dark blue "MOBILGAS" in center band.

Mobilgas—green lettering w/red line
(5) 1932–1933 15" Metal L/H Red $500–800
White globe face with thin red line positioned above and below center, forming a white band across the center of globe face. Bright green "MOBILGAS" in center band.

Mobilgas—blue lettering w/red line & horse
(6) 1933–1934 15" Metal L/H Red No Listing
White globe face with thin red line positioned above and below center, forming a white band across the center of

globe face. Dark blue "MOBILGAS" in center band. Small red flying horse center above upper red line.

Mobilgas Ethyl
(3) 1928–1933 16.5" Metal L/H Red $325–575
Mobilgas Ethyl
(3) 1928–1933 15" Metal L/H Red $325–575
White globe face with small Ethyl (EGC) logo at top of globe face. Black "MOBILGAS" across center above black "ETHYL."

Mobilgas Ethyl
(3) 1930–1933 16.5" Metal L/H Red $325–575
Mobilgas Ethyl
(3) 1930–1933 15" Metal L/H Red $325–575
Mobilgas Ethyl (red Ethyl)
(4) 1930–1933 13.5" Glass W $250–375
White globe face with small Ethyl (EGC) logo at top of globe face. Dark blue "MOBILGAS" across center above red "ETHYL."

Mobilgas Ethyl (black Ethyl)
(4) 1930–1933 13.5" Glass W $250–375
White globe face with small Ethyl (EGC) logo at top of globe face. Dark blue "MOBILGAS" across center above black "ETHYL."

Gargoyle Mobiloil (large)
(3) 1920–1935 OPC Oval $1,750–2,250
Oval one–piece cast globe with red outline ring. Detailed red and black Gargoyle logo with black "GARGOYLE" arched over top of logo. Black "MOBILOIL" across lower globe face below logo.

Gargoyle Mobiloil (small; raised border)
(3) 1920–1935 OPC Oval $1,750–2,250
Smaller globe similar to above with red recessed outline ring. Oval one–piece cast globe with red outline ring. Detailed red and black Gargoyle logo with black "GARGOYLE" arched over top of logo. Black "MOBILOIL" across lower globe face below logo.

Gargoyle Mobiloil (small; recessed border)
(3) 1920–1935 OPC Oval $1,750–2,250
Smaller globe similar to above with red recessed outline ring. Oval one–piece cast globe with red outline ring. Detailed red and black Gargoyle logo with black "GARGOYLE" arched over top of logo. Black "MOBILOIL" across lower globe face below logo.

Gargoyle Mobiloil porcelain sign globe
(3) 1920–1935 OPC Oval No Listing
Oval porcelain sign globe with Gargoyle Mobiloil logo similar to that used on glass globes. Two-sided porcelain, with globe-type base.

As a companion to Mobilgas, Socony-Vacuum introduced the premium grade Mobilgas Special in 1936. While several of the affiliated companies retained their individual brand names for premium grade gasoline until the 1940s, this Mobilgas Special three-piece glass globe was found on pumps from 1936 until 1962. *Dave Mercer collection, PCM archives*

Gargoyle Mobiloil
(6) 1930s 16.5" Metal HP Red $1,800–2,500
White globe face with black "Mobiloil" logotype across lower center of globe face. Red and black detailed Gargoyle logo on upper center of globe face with black "GARGOYLE" arched across top. Lettering of "GARGOYLE" has red line arching through center of lettering.

Lubrite Refining Co.
St. Louis, Missouri

An early refiner/marketer that was a pioneer in the development of service stations in the Midwest, Lubrite was purchased by Vacuum Oil Company in 1929 to greatly expand its growing presence with the Mobilgas brand.

Lubrite
(6) 1925–1929 15" Metal HP Red $600–900
White globe face with blue outlined red "Lubrite" logotype across center of globe face.
Lubrite Sky High
(6) 1925–1929 15" Metal HP Red $650–950

Mobiloil, the original aftermarket motor oil, was sold from special cabinets that were placed on pump islands and identified by this cast oval "Gargoyle Mobiloil" globe displayed proudly on top. *Dave Mercer collection, PCM archives*

White globe face with red "Lubrite" logotype across upper center of globe face. Large tapering blue "SKY–HY" with speed lines across lower globe face.

Wadhams Oil Corporation
Milwaukee, Wisconsin

Founded in the 1870s as a lubricants manufacturer, Wadhams was a pioneer in gasoline marketing, operating Wadhams stations throughout Wisconsin prior to 1920. Wadhams was briefly affiliated with the Independent Oil Men of America about 1925 and expanded with the 1929 purchase of Milwaukee competitor Bartles-McGuire Oil Company.

Noted for its Chinese pagoda-style stations, Wadhams had developed a first-class gasoline marketing organization when the company was purchased by Vacuum in 1930. Vacuum's Mobilgas trademark was added to the Wadhams brands and finally replaced the Wadhams name about 1939.

"W" Lamppost globe
(5) 1910s   OPE $900–1,200
Unusual vase-shaped white glass lamppost globe with a large red "W" on opposite sides of view.

Wadhams w/can
(6) 1910s   OPE   No Listing
White globe with black "WADHAMS" and red gasoline can on globe face.

Wadhams True Gasoline
(6) 1910s   OPE   No Listing
White globe with red "WADHAMS (large "W") across center of globe face. Small black "TRUE GASOLINE" below "WADHAMS."

Wadhams 370 w/can
(6) 1920–1922   15" Metal   HP   No Listing
White globe face with black "WADHAMS" across top. Red "370" with black drop shadow arched across center. Detailed red and black gasoline carry can at bottom of globe face.

Wadhams SpeciaLo
(5) 1920–1922   15" Metal   HP $1,700–2,250
White globe face with black "WADHAMS" across top. Red "SpeciaLo" with black drop shadow arched across center. Detailed red and black gasoline carry can at bottom of globe face.

Wadhams 370 Steel Face
(5) 1922–1925   15" Metal   HP $900–1,250
White reflective steel face with black "WADHAMS" across top. Red "370" with black drop shadow across center over red circle. Black "W" on red band below.

Wadhams 370
(5) 1922–1925   15" Metal   HP $800–1,100
White globe face with black "WADHAMS" across top. Red "370" with black drop shadow across center over red circle. Black "W" on red band below.

Wadhams Anti-Knock Steel Face
(4) 1922–1925   15" Metal   HP $900–1,250
White reflective steel face with black "WADHAMS" across top. Red "ANTI-KNOCK" with black drop shadow arched across center over red bar. Black "W" superimposed over red bar.

Wadhams Red Hat
(9) 1925–1926   15" Metal   HP   No Listing
White globe with black outline ring around globe face. Large red top hat with black hat band in center of globe. Three white stars on black hat band. Small black triangle/red thunderbird IOMA logo below hat. Black "WADHAMS" arched around top, "GASOLINE" around bottom with "RED" to left of hat and "HAT" to right.

Wadhams "Independent" IOMA
(5) 1926–1929   15" Metal   HP $1,200–1,600
White globe face with red outline ring. Red semicircle at top of globe face. Black "Wadhams" across center with black triangle/red thunderbird IOMA logo at bottom of globe face.

Wadhams Ethyl (EGC)
(4) 1926–1932   15" Metal   HP $750–950
White globe face with red outline ring. Yellow "bar" with black "W" at top of globe face. Black "Wadhams " across center with large black and red outlined white circle on lower globe face. Large Ethyl (EGC) logo in circle.

Wadhams Mobilgas
(5) 1929–1932   15" Metal   HP $900–1,300
Red globe face with series of increasing-width white horizontal lines above and below white center band. Black "MOBILGAS" across white center band. Black "Wadhams" in upper red area above "Mobilgas."

Wadhams Metro "W"+
(4) 1929–1932   15" Metal   HP $600–900
White globe face with yellow outline ring. Black "Wadhams" across upper globe face above large black "METRO." Red "bar" with black "W" on lower globe face.

Wadhams Mobilgas w/shield
(6) 1932–1935   13.5" Glass   W   No Listing
Red globe face with series of increasing-width white horizontal lines above and below white center band. Black "MOBILGAS" across white center band. Black "Wadhams" in upper red area above "Mobilgas." Small black outlined white shield emblem just below "Mobilgas" with small flying red horse in shield.

Wadhams Metro "W"
(4) 1932–1940   13.5" Glass   W $300–500
White globe face with yellow outline ring. Black "Wadhams" across upper globe face above large black "METRO." Red "bar" with black "W" on lower globe face.

Wadhams Giant
(5) 1932–1940   13.5" Glass   W $300–550
White globe face with red outline ring. Black "Wadhams" across upper globe face with red "GIANT" with black drop shadow arched across center. Red "bar" with black "W" on lower globe face.

Wadhams Ethyl
(3) 1932–1940   13.5" Glass   W $300–550
White globe face with red outline ring. Red "bar" with black "W" at top of globe face over black "Wadhams." Black/yellow/black outlined white circle on lower globe face with large Ethyl (EGC) logo on circle.

Bartles-McGuire Oil Company
Milwaukee, Wisconsin

Large Wisconsin marketer that merged with Wadhams in 1929, shortly before Vacuum purchased Wadhams.

Bartles White Eagle Gasoline
(6) 1920s   OPE Oval   No Listing
White oval one-piece etched globe with small eagle design in center. Red band across center with white "WHITE" to left of eagle and "EAGLE" to right. Black "BARTLES" arched around top, "GASOLINE" around bottom.

Bartles Bonded Gasoline
(5) 1921–1929 15" Metal $650–950
White globe face with large red "B" covering most of globe face. Red arrow diagonal through "B." White "BARTLES" in upper area of "B," "BONDED" in lower area with white "GASOLINE" on diagonal arrow.

White Star Refining Co.
Detroit, Michigan

Also added to Vacuum's Mobilgas marketing was Detroit's White Star Refining. White Star operated more than 1,500 stations in Ohio, Indiana, and Michigan when purchased by Vacuum in 1930. Mobilgas replaced the White Star brand almost immediately, but former White Star outlets used a special Mobilgas shield sign with a small blue circle and white star at the bottom until after World War II.

White Star Gasoline
(6) 1918–1920 OPE   W $2,200–2,800
White globe with blue globe face. Large white star in center with blue band across center of star. White "WHITE STAR/GASOLINE" on center band with white "WHITE STAR REFINING CO." arched around top and "A/QUALITY/PRODUCT" below star.

White Star Etched Milk Glass Faces
(5) 1918–1920 15" Metal   L/H $2,200–2,800
Blue globe face with large white star in center. Blue band across star with white "WHITE STAR/GASOLINE" on band. White "WHITE STAR REFINING CO." arched around top, "A/QUALITY/PRODUCT" below star.

White Star Gasoline
(6) 1918–1920 15" Metal   L/H $900–1,250
Blue globe face. Large white star in center with blue band across center of star. White "WHITE STAR/GASOLINE" on center band with white "WHITE STAR REFINING CO." arched around top and "A/QUALITY/PRODUCT" below star.

Staroline Gasoline is Better
(6) 1918–1920 15" Metal   L/H $900–1,250
Blue globe face. Large white star in center with blue band across star's center. White script "Staroline" on center band with white "WHITE STAR REFINING CO." arched around top and "GASOLINE/IS BETTER" below star.

White Star Gasoline
(5) 1918–1920 15" Metal   L/H $900–1,250
White globe face with blue circle in center. Blue "WHITE STAR" arched around top. "GASOLINE" around bottom. Large white star in blue center circle with blue logotype "Staroline" above "MOTOR/OILS" on star.

Staroline Better Gasoline
(4) 1920–1922 15" Metal   L/H $900–1,250
Blue globe face with white outline ring. White script logotype "Staroline" arched across top above small "BETTER." White "GASOLINE" arched around bottom.

Staroline Gasoline Is Better
(4) 1922–1926 15" Metal   L/H $900–1,250
Blue globe face with white outline ring. Small white outlined blue circle with white star at top. Script white "Staroline" across center with white "GASOLINE/IS BETTER" below.

White Star Gasoline
(4) 1926–1930 15" Metal   L/H $850–1,200
Blue globe face with white outline around blue center circle. White star in center circle with white "WHITE STAR" arched around top and "GASOLINE" around bottom.

White Star Ethyl
(5) 1926–1930 15" Metal   L/H $650–900
Blue globe face with white/blue outlined white center circle. Large Ethyl (EGC) logo in center circle. White "WHITE STAR" arched around top, "GASOLINE" around bottom.

Staroline and White Star Ethyl
(5) 1926–1930 15" Metal   L/H $750–1,000
Blue globe face with small white circle at top. Small Ethyl (EGC) logo in circle. White script "Staroline" across center above small white "AND" above white "WHITE STAR." Yellow "ETHYL" below "WHITE STAR."

White Star Gasoline
(5) 1930–1934 15" Metal   L/H $900–1,250
White globe face with red circle in center. White star in red center circle. Blue "WHITE STAR" arched around top, "GASOLINE" around bottom.

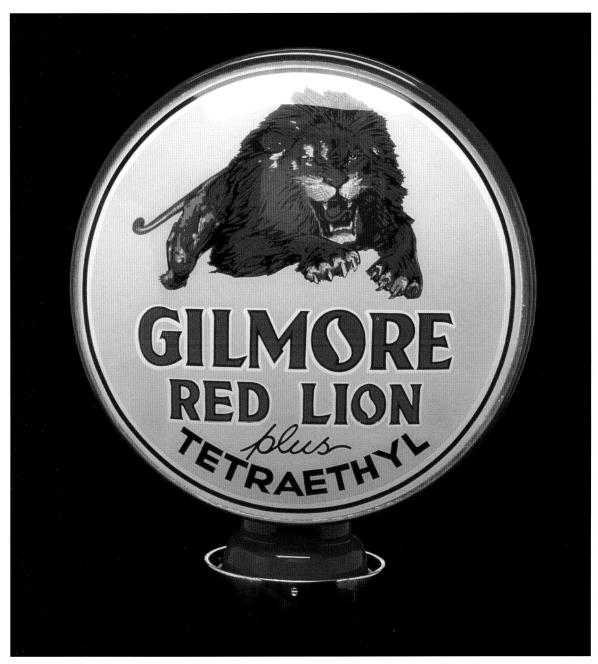

Mobil's purchase of Gilmore and elimination of the brand name at the end of World War II spelled the end of beautiful Gilmore advertising items such as this rare Gilmore Red Lion metal band globe. *Dave Mercer collection, PCM archives*

White Star Gasoline
(5) 1930–1934 15" Metal L/H $900–1,250
Red globe face with blue circle in center. White star in blue circle. White "WHITE STAR" arched around top, "GASOLINE" around bottom.

White Star Staroline Motor Oils (no star)
(6) 1930s 15" Metal L/H No Listing
Description not available.

White Star Oil Co. of Canada

The Canadian affiliate of Detroit's White Star Refining Company.

Starlite Gasoline
(6) 1920s 15" Metal HP No Listing
Description not available.

One of the original consumer brand names for gasoline, Socony used an elaborate monogram and shield logo from the early teens until the merger with Socony-Vacuum in 1932. Notice that the shield design on this metal band globe matches the shield design used for many years in Mobilgas signage. *Dave Mercer collection, PCM archives*

White Star Hi Test
(6) 1920s   15" Metal   HP $900–1,250
Blue globe face with large white/red outlined white star in center. Red "HIGH/TEST" on star. White outlined black "WHITE STAR" arched around top of globe face, "OIL" to left of star, "CO." to right and "GAS" arched around bottom.

Independent Oil Co. of Pennsylvania
Altoona, Pennsylvania

Purchased by Socony-Vacuum in 1934 and rebranded Mobilgas.

Independent (w/three men)
(4) 1925–1934 15" Metal HP $3,500–5,000
White globe face with dark green "INDEPENDENT" arched around top. Dark green outlined white circle on lower globe face with multi-color scene with colonial soldiers and drummer.

Independent Ethyl (EGC)
(6) 1925–1934 15" Metal HP $400–600
White globe face with dark green "INDEPENDENT" arched around top. Dark green outlined white circle on lower globe face with Ethyl (EGC) logo with rays in circle.

Independent Gasoline (w/three men; great detail)
(5) 1925–1934 15" Metal HP No Listing
Yellow globe face with dark green outlined white circle in center. Multicolored scene with colonial soldiers and drummer in center circle. Dark green "INDEPEN-DENT" arched around top, "GASOLINE" around bottom. This globe was produced with a painted, nonbaked finish. Though a few are known to exist, only one is known to be in presentable condition today. No attempt will be made to price that one example. If more are found, they would be worth several thousand dollars.

Independent Gasoline (w/three men; less detail)
(6) 1925–1934 15" Metal HP No Listing
Yellow globe face with dark green outlined white circle in center. Less detailed multicolored scene with colonial soldiers and drummer in center circle. Dark green "IN-DEPENDENT" arched around top, "GASOLINE" around bottom.

Metro
Jamestown/Olean, New York

Small New York marketer purchased by Socony-Vacuum in 1934. The Mobilgas brand was added at Metro stations (note the red/white/green "Mobilgas" globe in the Vacuum section) and Metro became a mo-tor-grade product sold at Mobil stations in the various marketing territories until after World War II.

This rare can-shaped light globe advertising Mobiloil motor oil dates from the late 1940s. *Lonnie Hop collection*

Metro w/diamond
(6) 1920s   15" Metal   No Listing
Description not available.

Metro Ethyl
(6) 1920s   15" Metal   No Listing
Description not available.

Metro 68–70
(6) 1920s   15" Metal   No Listing
Description not available.

Metro Gasoline/green lines
(4) 1925–1933 15" Metal $400–650
White globe face with thin green line positioned above and below center. Large green "METRO" over smaller green "GASOLINE" between the lines across center of globe face.

Metro Gas Gargoyle Mobiloil
(5) 1933–1935 16.5" Metal $2,200–2,700
Metro Gas Gargoyle Mobiloil
(5) 1933–1935 15" Metal $2,200–2,700
White globe face with red/white/blue lines across center. Blue "Metro" arched over "Gas" on upper half, red and black Gargoyle logo with black "GARGOYLE" with red

Prior to its merger with Socony, Vacuum marketed under the Mobilgas brand in several states in the East and Upper Midwest. This globe advertised their Ethyl product in this era.

stripe arched above over black "Mobiloil" on lower globe face.
Metro green/green on white/green
(3) 1935–1940 16.5" Metal $400–650
Metro green/green on white/green
(3) 1935–1940 15" Metal $400–650
Metro green/green on white/green
(3) 1935–1940 13.5" Glass   W $250–400
Green globe face with white band across center. Large green "METRO" over smaller green "GASOLINE" on center band.

Metro red/green on white/red
(2) 1940–1955 15" Metal $400–650
Metro red/green on white/red
(2) 1940–1955 13.5" Glass   W   No Listing
Metro red/green on white/red
(2) 1940–1955 Capco $175–275
Red globe face with white band across center. Red outlined green "Metro" across center on white band.
Metro red/black on white/red (General)
(5) 1930–1935 16.5" Metal $450–700

Red globe face with white band across center. Red outlined black "Metro" across center on white band.

Gilmore Oil Co.
Los Angeles, California
Founded in 1900, Gilmore entered gasoline marketing in 1923. The company established an elaborate network of dealers in California, Oregon, and Washington, totaling more than 3,500 outlets at its peak in the late 1930s. In 1940 Socony-Vacuum purchased control of Gilmore and assigned Gilmore marketing to the General Petroleum subsidiary. Transition from the Gilmore brand to Mobilgas began in 1942 and was completed in 1945, just after World War II.

Note that Gilmore globes are often bought, sold, and traded as single inserts because of their expense. Some prices were determined by combining two single insert prices with the value for a body and assembly.

Gilmore "Roar With Gilmore"
(4) 1925–1942 15" Metal   HP Red $7,000–9,000
Yellow globe face with black outline ring. Large red and black jumping lion at top of face with black "ROAR" over black script "With" beside lion. Black outlined red "GILMORE" over black and white checkered flag below lion.

Gilmore Blu-Green Gasoline
(4) 1925–1933 15" Metal   HP Red $8,000–11,000
Yellow globe face with black outline ring and black outlines around white semicircles in center. Large multicolor lion's head in center superimposed over semicircles. Black outlined red "GILMORE" arched around top, "GASOLINE" around bottom with blue "BLU" to left of lion and "GREEN" to right.

Gilmore With Ethyl (block letters)
(5) 1926–1942 15" Metal   HP Red $2,000–3,500
Yellow globe face with black outline ring around white center circle. Small Ethyl (EGC) logo with red rays in center circle with black BLOCK "With" above. Black outlined red "GILMORE" arched around top, "GASOLINE" around bottom.

Gilmore With Ethyl (script letters)
(5) 1926–1942 15" Metal   HP Red $2,000–3,500
Yellow globe face with black outline ring around white center circle. Small Ethyl (EGC) logo with red rays in center circle with black SCRIPT "With" above. Black outlined red "GILMORE" arched around top, "GASOLINE" around bottom.

Gilmore Red Lion w/Tetraethyl
(4) 1933–1942 15" Metal   HP Red $8,000–10,000
Yellow globe face with black outline ring. Large red and

black lion at top of globe face. Black outlined red "GILMORE/RED LION" over black script "plus" with black "TETRAETHYL" arched around bottom.
Gilmore Fleet w/flag
(6) 1933–1942 15" Metal   HP Red   No Listing
Yellow globe face with black outline ring. Black outlined red "GILMORE" across center over italic black "FLEET." Small black and white checkered flag at top of globe face.

Clipper Oil Company
Seattle, Washington

Exact history unknown, believed to have been purchased by Mobil in the 1950s and continued as a secondary brand into the 1960s.

Clipper w/airplane
(4) 1940s   15" Metal $3,000–4,500
White globe face with green/red airplane in center of globe face. Red "CLIPPER" with green drop shadow and speed lines across lower globe face.

Clipper w/airplane
(4) 1940s   Oval Capco $1,100–1,600
White globe face with green/red airplane in center of globe face. Red "CLIPPER" with green drop shadow and speed lines across lower globe face.

Mobilgas/Socony-Vacuum

As noted in the introduction, Socony and Vacuum merged in 1931. By 1934 it was decided to join the Socony shield and flying horse with Vacuum's Mobilgas to create a single brand name for all the affiliates. Several, including Magnolia and White Eagle, readily converted to the new Mobilgas identity. Others, including General and Wadhams, combined the Mobilgas brand with their own brand names, at least for the first few years. Conversion was nearly complete when World War II interrupted business, and it was completed as soon as possible after the war.

Please note, however, that many manufacturers were involved in making the following globes and color variations—including some certain to exist but not listed—exist as well as typestyle and size variations. A complete listing would be nearly impossible, but two years of research has compiled the following list.

Note also that there are no differences in value between black and blue lettering, so if your globe is not listed, the value can be determined by comparing it with the same globe with the other color lettering. The "Mobilgas" designation for products was changed to Mobil in 1962 and all of the older globes were replaced at that time.

Mobilgas with horse black letters
(4) 1934–1962 16.5" Metal L/H Red $500–750
Mobilgas with horse black letters
(4) 1934–1962 15" Metal   L/H Red $500–750

The brandname Metro was inherited when Socony-Vacuum purchased New York marketer Metro. It remained in use until the 1950s as Mobil's motor grade gasoline. This Metro globe is from the 1930s.

Mobilgas with horse black letters
(4) 1934–1962 13.5" Glass   WN $300–500
White globe face with flying red horse at top of globe face. Black "Mobilgas" across lower globe face.
Mobilgas with horse blue letters
(2) 1934–1962 16.5" Metal L/H Red $500–750
Mobilgas with horse blue letters
(2) 1934–1962 15" Metal   L/H Red $500–750
Mobilgas with horse blue letters
(2) 1934–1962 13.5" Glass   WN $300–500
Mobilgas with horse blue letters
(4) 1934–1962 Gill $350–550
Mobilgas with horse blue letters
(5) 1934–1962 Balcrank $400–650
Mobilgas with horse blue letters
(2) 1955–1962 Capco $200–400
White globe face with flying red horse at top of globe face. Blue "Mobilgas" across lower globe face.

Mobilgas Ethyl with horse
(4) 1934–1936 Gill $375–575
Mobilgas Ethyl with horse
(4) 1934–1936 15" Metal   L/H Red $550–800

Mobilgas Ethyl with horse
(4) 1934–1936 13.5" Glass   WN $325–525
White globe face with flying red horse at top. Black "Mobilgas" over red "ETHYL" on lower globe face.

Mobilgas Special black letters
(4) 1936–1962 16.5" Metal   L/H Red $500–750
Mobilgas Special black letters
(4) 1936–1962 15" Metal   L/H Red $500–750
Mobilgas Special black letters
(4) 1936–1962 13.5" Glass   WN $300–500
White globe face with flying red horse at top of globe face. Black "Mobilgas" over red "SPECIAL" on lower globe face.

Mobilgas Special blue letters
(2) 1936–1962 16.5" Metal   L/H Red $500–750
Mobilgas Special blue letters
(2) 1936–1962 15" Metal   L/H Red $500–750
Mobilgas Special blue letters
(2) 1936–1962 13.5" Glass   WN $300–500
Mobilgas Special blue letters
(4) 1936–1962 Gill $350–550
Mobilgas Special blue letters
(5) 1936–1962 Balcrank $400–650
Mobilgas Special blue letters
(2) 1955–1962 Capco $200–400
White globe face with flying red horse at top. Blue "Mobilgas" over red "SPECIAL" on lower globe face.

Mobilgas Special large "Special"
(4) 1946–1950 13.5" Glass   WN $325–525
Mobilgas Special large "Special"
(4) 1946–1950 Gill $375–575
White globe face with small flying red horse at top. Small blue "Mobilgas" over large red "SPECIAL" on lower globe face.

Mobilgas/Mobilgas Special dual
(5) 1955–1962 Capco   No Listing
White globe face with small flying red horse at top. Thin blue line across center of globe with blue vertical line down from midpoint of horizontal line. Blue "Mobilgas" to one side of vertical line with red arrow pointing down diagonal with blue "Mobilgas" over red "SPECIAL" with red arrow on other side of vertical line. Note that faces would be opposite for opposite sides of the pump. Very rare globe for 1950s dual pump.

Mobilfuel Diesel black letters
(4) 1935–1962 15" Metal   L/H Red $800–1,100
Mobilfuel Diesel black letters
(4) 1935–1962 13.5" Glass   WN $500–800
White globe face with flying red horse at top. Black "Mobilfuel" over red "DIESEL" on lower globe face.

Mobilfuel Diesel blue letters
(4) 1935–1962 16.5" Metal   L/H Red $800–1,100
Mobilfuel Diesel blue letters
(4) 1935–1962 15" Metal   L/H Red $800–1,100
Mobilfuel Diesel blue letters
(4) 1935–1962 13.5" Glass   WN $500–800
Mobilfuel Diesel blue letters
(4) 1935–1962 Capco $450–600
White globe face with flying red horse at top. Blue "Mobilfuel" over red "DIESEL" on lower globe face.

Mobilfuel Diesel Special blue letters
(4) 1935–1962 16.5" Metal   L/H Red $850–1,200
Mobilfuel Diesel Special blue letters
(4) 1935–1962 15" Metal   L/H Red $850–1,200
White globe face with flying red horse at top. Blue "Mobilfuel" over red "DIESEL SPECIAL" on lower globe face.

Mobilgas Marine with non–outlined horse
(6) 1930s   16.5" Metal   L/H Red $1,000–1,500
White globe face with flying red horse at top. Early locally made globe with poorly drawn horse. Black "Mobilgas" over red "MARINE" on lower globe face.

Mobilgas Marine with horse
(4) 1950–1962 15" Metal   L/H Red $1,000–1,500
Mobilgas Marine with horse
(4) 1950–1962 13.5" Glass   WN $750–1,000
White globe face with flying red horse at top. Black "Mobilgas" over red "MARINE" on lower globe face.

Mobilgas Marine White with horse
(6) 1950–1962 15" Metal   L/H Red $1,200–1,750
White globe face with flying red horse at top. Blue "Mobilgas" over red "MARINE WHITE" on lower globe face.

Aero Mobilgas with horse
(5) 1935–1950 15" Metal   L/H Red $1,800–2,400
White globe face with flying red horse at top. Blue "AERO" offset to left over blue "Mobilgas."

Mobilgas Aircraft with horse
(4) 1935–1962 16.5" Metal   L/H Red $1,500–2,000
Mobilgas Aircraft with horse
(4) 1935–1962 15" Metal   L/H Red $1,500–2,000
Mobilgas Aircraft with horse
(4) 1935–1962 13.5" Glass   WN $900–1,300
White globe face with flying red horse at top. Black "Mobilgas" over red "AIRCRAFT" on lower globe face.

Mobilgas Aircraft italic letters
(5) 1935–1962 13.5" Glass   WN $950–1,350
White globe face with flying red horse at top. Blue "Mobilgas" over italic red "AIRCRAFT" on lower globe face.

Stove/Mobilheat/Oils
(5) 1940–1955 16.5" Metal   L/H Red $900–1,400
Stove/Mobilheat/Oils
(5) 1940–1955 15" Metal   L/H Red $900–1,400
White globe face with black "Mobilheat" across center. Red "STOVE" above "Mobilheat," "OILS" below.

Mobilheat Stove Oil with no outline horse
(5) 1955–1962 13.5" Glass   WN $750–1,000
White globe face with flying red horse at top. *No* outline around horse. Blue "Mobilheat" above red "STOVE OIL" on lower globe face.

Mobilheat Stove Oil with horse
(5) 1955–1962 Capco $450–700
White globe face with flying red outlined horse at top. Blue "Mobilheat" above red "STOVE OIL" on lower globe face.

Kerosene with horse
(6) 1940s   15" Metal   L/H Red No Listing
White globe face with flying red horse at top. Blue "KEROSENE" on lower globe face.

Mobil/Kerosene with horse
(5) 1950–1966 15" Metal   L/H Red $750–1,000
Mobil/Kerosene with horse
(4) 1950–1966 13.5" Glass   WN $500–800
Mobil/Kerosene with horse
(5) 1950–1966 Capco $300–500
White globe face with blue outlined flying red horse positioned upper right of center. Blue "Mobil/ Kerosene" positioned lower right.

Mobiloil (can-shaped globe)
(6) 1947–1955 OPP   No Listing
Cylindrically shaped white glass globe. Upper area had flying red horse above blue "Mobiloil"; lower third is covered by red band. Shaped and imaged in the likeness of the 1947 Mobiloil motor oil can.

Mobil

Although the Mobil name gradually replaced Mobilgas as the primary station identification between 1955 and 1958, gasoline brands remained Mobilgas and Mobilgas Special until 1962, when they were replaced with Mobil Regular and Mobil Premium. Mobil again reimaged in 1966, replacing the elongated Mobil shield with the modern "red O" logo. No U.S. globes with the 1966 logo are known to exist.

Mobil Regular
(2) 1962–1966 Capco $200–300
White globe face with red/white/blue "1958" flat "Mobil" shield above "Regular" in blue.

Mobil Premium
(2) 1962–1966 Capco $200–300
White globe face with red/white/blue "1958" flat "Mobil" shield above "Premium" in red.

Mobilfuel Diesel
(4) 1962–1966 Capco $250–350
White globe face with red/white/blue "1958" flat "Mobil" shield above "Mobilfuel/Diesel" in blue.

Mobil Signs

@ long with the use of gas pump globes, Socony enhanced its image with elaborate signage. In the early years, when gasoline was dispensed from curb pumps, signage was limited to a flanged sign mounted on the front of the store. These projecting signs served to identify the brand of petroleum products offered in the days when many marketers still used generic "Gasoline" globes supplied by pump manufacturers. In the following listings you will see several examples of Socony flange signs and other early identification signs. Vacuum, too, used flanged signs extensively; indeed, the Gargoyle Mobiloil signs are among the most popular and most commonly found. Each of the other affiliated companies had distinctive signage, of note in particular are the many beautiful and rare signs used by Gilmore.

From the mid-1930s onward, the Mobil affiliates used many variations of the Mobilgas shields, and their unique die-cut shape makes them extremely popular among collectors. Also from this era—and perhaps among the most popular signs from any brand—are the various Mobil die-cut flying horses, found in flat, embossed, and high relief designs.

Mobil Signs Listings

Listings for Mobil signs provide information about size, rarity, years the signs were used, and their price range.

Size

Approximate dimensions are given in inches, with the horizontal length listed first, followed by the vertical measure (i.e., 26x30). Single numerals (36") indicate the diameter of round signs in inches.

Service stations offering a particular product often advertised the fact with small lollipop-shaped signs that were placed at curbside. The Gargoyle Mobiloil curb sign was one of the most familiar. Mobil used curb signs to advertise Mobiloil as late as the 1960s. *Dave Mercer collection, PCM archives*

One of the most familiar signs of the first 35 years of this century is this porcelain flanged Gargoyle Mobiloil sign.

Rarity Code

A numerical code system—which has been expanded since the Texaco collectibles book was published—can be interpreted as follows:

(1): A very common sign that's readily available in collector circles.

(2): A common sign; fairly readily available among collectors.

(3): Available. These signs, though available, are a little more scarce.

(4): Rare—few are known to exist. They are around but are much harder to find.

(5): Extremely rare; fewer than 10 are known to exist; rarely found or offered for sale.

Years Used

The years are those the sign would have been placed in service in a new installation. In practice many items remained in use long after they had been officially replaced.

Mobiloil enjoyed an excellent reputation in European markets, where it was advertised to the motoring public at garages that displayed signs like the one shown here. *Dave Mercer collection, PCM archives*

Price Range

The prices in this book are listed as a range—from wholesale to retail. Ranges are left between the two prices to allow for variations in condition, negotiation, etc. A price of $1,500–2,200 simply means that $1,500 is a wholesale value and $2,200 is the top retail value. Both are considered good deals within their respective definitions.

Socony
Identification Signs
We Sell Socony Motor Gasoline
26x30   (5)   1915–1931 $850
Blue porcelain sign with SONY logo in center. Blue outlined white strip across top and white outlined blue strip across bottom. Red "WE SELL" across upper white area and white "STANDARD OIL CO of N.Y." across lower blue area.

Socony Gasoline/Motor Oil shield
42x48   (4)   1924–1931 $650
Blue outlined white porcelain shield with red "SOCONY" across top. Blue "GASOLINE/ MOTOR OIL" across center with smaller red "STANDARD OIL CO." below. Red "OF NEW YORK" arched around bottom.

Socony Socony-Vacuum shield
36"   (4)   1932–1946 $650
Socony Socony-Vacuum shield
48"   (3)   1932–1946 $550

Blue outlined white porcelain five-point shield. Blue "SOCONY" across bottom of shield with red "SOCONY-VACUUM" below. Blue outlined flying red horse covers top of shield area.

Pump Signs
Socony Gasoline
10x15   (5)   1915–1922 $250
Blue outlined white flat porcelain sign with blue "SOCONY/GASOLINE" across sign. Red "UNIFORM QUALITY" above, "BEST RESULTS" below.

Socony Gasoline
10x15   (5)   1915–1922 $225
Blue outlined white curved porcelain sign with blue "SOCONY/GASOLINE" across sign. Red "UNIFORM QUALITY" above, "BEST RESULTS" below.

Ask for Socony Motor Oil flat
15x15   (4)   1915–1922 $250
Blue/red outlined white flat porcelain sign with blue "ask for/SOCONY/MOTOR/OIL" on sign face.

Ask for Socony Motor Oil curved
15x15   (4)   1915–1922 $225
Blue/red outlined white curved porcelain sign with blue "Ask for/SOCONY/MOTOR/OIL" on sign face.

Ask for Socony Parabase Motor Oil
10x15   (4)   1926–1930 $300
Blue outlined white flat porcelain sign with blue "ASK FOR/SOCONY" across top. Red script "Parabase" above blue "MOTOR/OIL" below "SOCONY."

Ask for Socony Parabase Motor Oil
10x15   (4)   1926–1930 $275
Blue outlined white curved porcelain sign with blue "ASK FOR/SOCONY" across top. Red script "Parabase" above blue "MOTOR/OIL" below "SOCONY."

Socony Winter Ethyl
10x16   (4)   1928–1930 $650
Die-cut pennant-shaped white tin litho sign. Black script "Socony" above black "WINTER/ETHYL" across pennant.

Curb Signs
Stop Here Socony Motor Oil
24"   (2)   1918–1930 $450
White porcelain sign with blue outlined red "SOCONY" across center. Blue "MOTOR/OIL" below "SOCONY," "Stop Here" above.

Lubrication/Motor Oil Signs

Socony Motor Oils
10x15   (5)   1915–1920 $250
White outlined blue porcelain sign with white "SO-CONY/MOTOR/OILS" across sign face.

Socony Chassis Lubricant
18x30   (3)   1915–1925 $225
Red/white outlined blue porcelain sign with white "SO-CONY" across top. Red "CHASSIS" in white band in center. White "LUBRICANT/(PRESSURE GUN GREASE)" below band.

Crank Case Service Socony Motor Oil
32x26   (3)   1920–1925 $350
Red/white outlined blue porcelain sign with white "Crank Case Service" across top. Red "Drain and Refill with" across center and white "SOCONY MOTOR OIL" across bottom.

Socony Air-Craft Oils
12x20   (4)   1925–1932 $1,500
Socony Air-Craft Oils
20x30   (3)   1925–1931 $1,200
Red/white outlined blue porcelain sign with white "SO-CONY" across top and white "OILS" across bottom. Small white "STANDARD OIL COMPANY OF NEW YORK" across bottom edge. Blue and white detailed airplane in center with red "AIRCRAFT" across single white upper wing.

Lubester Signs

SONY Socony Motor Oil shield
15"   (4)   1915–1931 $800
Blue/red outlined blue curved porcelain sign with red outlined white shield on lower sign face. Large white "SONY" wraps around shield. Red "SOCONY" across upper shield with blue "MOTOR/OIL" below. Blue "Standard Oil Company of New York" arched around bottom.

Front SONY Socony Motor Oil shield
15"   (3)   1915–1931 $950
Blue/red outlined blue flat porcelain sign with red outlined white shield on lower sign face. Large white "SONY" wraps around shield. Red "SOCONY" across upper shield with blue "MOTOR/OIL" below. Blue "Standard Oil Company of New York" arched around bottom.

SONY oval shield
10x16   (4)   1920–1925 $600
Blue porcelain rectangular sign with distorted SONY shield in white oval in center.

SONY Socony Motor Oil
8x9.5   (4)   1915–1931   All $550

One of the earliest engine oils designed specifically for aviation use was Socony Air-Craft Oil. These signs advertised the product where it could be purchased. *Dave Mercer collection, PCM archives*

Blue/white outlined blue flat porcelain sign with red outlined white shield on lower sign face. Large white "SONY" wraps around shield. Red "SOCONY" across upper shield with blue "MOTOR/OIL" below. Blue "Standard Oil Company of New York" arched around bottom. Blue outlined white base with grade listing in red across white area. The following grade listings are known: LIGHT MEDIUM, MEDIUM, and 990 MOTOR OIL FOR FORD CARS.

SONY Socony Aircraft Oil
8x9.5   (4)   1915–1931   All $550
Blue/white outlined blue flat porcelain sign with red outlined white shield on lower sign face. Large white "SONY" wraps around shield. Red "SOCONY" across upper shield with red "AIRCRAFT" above blue "MOTOR/OIL" below. Blue "Standard Oil Company of New York" arched around bottom. Blue outlined white base with grade listing in red across white area. The following grade listings are known: LIGHT MEDIUM and MEDIUM.

Socony Parabase Motor Oil
8x9.5   (4)   1926–1932 $650
Blue outlined white porcelain keyhole-shaped sign with blue "SOCONY" above red script "Parabase" on upper sign face, Blue "MOTOR OIL" across center with blue grade name below. Blue "STANDARD OIL COMPANY OF NEW YORK" arched around bottom. Red grade information on lower keyhole area. The following grade is known: 990-A FOR FORD CARS.

Flange Signs

We Sell Socony Motor Gasoline
22x24   (3)   1915–1920 $950
This sign features an unusual version of the SONY shield

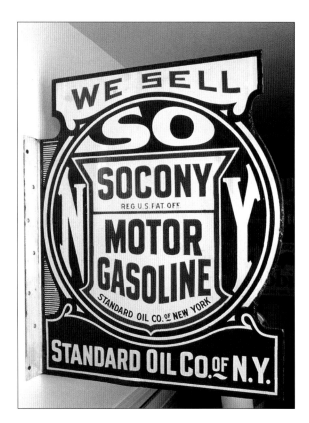

Main street in every New England town was incomplete without several merchants displaying this sign. Sold from bulk storage or curb pumps, this can be considered the earliest predecessor to today's high-rise or pylon-mounted Mobil station identification signs. *Dave Mercer collection, PCM archives*

logo: White outlined blue circle with a large white/blue outlined five-point shield positioned at lower edge of the circle. A pink band crosses the shield at the top with blue outlined red "MOTOR/GASOLINE" below the band. Small blue "STANDARD OIL CO. OF NEW YORK" around the bottom edge of the shield. Distorted white "S" and "O" in the blue area above the shield and elongated "N" to left and "Y" to the right of shield. Blue porcelain flange sign with SONY logo in center. Blue outlined area arched around top and white outlined blue strip across bottom. Red "WE SELL" across upper white area and white "STANDARD OIL CO. OF N.Y." across lower blue area.

We Sell Socony Motor Gasoline
22x24   (3)   1920–1931 $950
Blue porcelain flange sign with SONY logo in center. Blue outlined white strip across top and white outlined blue strip across bottom. Red "WE SELL" across upper white area and white "STANDARD OIL CO OF N.Y." across lower blue area.

Magnolia Petroleum
Dallas, Texas
Identification Signs
Magnolia Gasoline Motor Oil
42"   (4)   1918–1931 $1,250
White outlined red porcelain sign with white outlined blue center circle. White "MAGNOLIA" arched around top, "GASOLINE" around bottom. Small white magnolia flower with green leaves at top of center circle. Smaller flowers to either side of center on outer red band. White "MOTOR OIL" below flower in center.

Magnolia Mobilgas shield
48x48   (5)   1931–1936 $750
Blue outlined white porcelain five-point shield with blue "Mobilgas" (serif "a") across lower sign face above red "MAGNOLIA." Flying red horse logo at top of sign above "Mobilgas."

Curb Signs
Magnolia Petroleum Company Magnolia Gasoline for Sale Here
30"   (3)   1918–1925 $1,350
White outlined red porcelain sign with white outlined blue center circle. White "MAGNOLIA PETROLEUM" arched around top, "COMPANY" around bottom. Small white outlined red circle at top of center circle with white magnolia flower in center. White "MAGNOLIA/GASOLINE/ FOR SALE HERE" below flower on center circle.

Magnolia Petroleum Company Magnolene Motor Oils for Sale Here
30"   (4)   1918–1925 $1,350
White outlined red porcelain sign with white outlined blue center circle. White "MAGNOLIA PETROLEUM" arched around top, "COMPANY" around bottom. Small white outlined red circle at top of center circle with white magnolia flower in center. White script "Magnolene" above white "MOTOR OIL/FOR SALE HERE" below flower on center circle.

Magnolia Gasoline Magnolia Socony Motor Oil shield
30"   (4)   1925–1932 $1,500
White outlined red porcelain sign with white outlined blue center circle. White "MAGNOLIA" arched around top, "GASOLINE" around bottom. Small white "MAGNOLIA" above white/red outlined white five-point shield in center. Blue "SOCONY/MOTOR/OIL" on shield. White magnolia flower with green leaves to either side of shield in center.

Magnolia Ethyl Gasoline
30"   (4)   1926–1932 $750
White outlined red porcelain sign with white/blue outlined white center circle. White "MAGNOLIA" arched around

On the West Coast, Gilmore products were among the most popular and most heavily promoted. Signs such as this one were displayed by service stations and garages where Gilmore products were available. *Dave Mercer collection, PCM archives*

top, "GASOLINE" around bottom. Large Ethyl (EGC) logo with yellow rays in center.

Secondary Signs
Magnolia Gasoline for Sale Here
15x30   (5)   1918–1925 $650
Rectangular porcelain sign with red band across top, white band in center, and blue band across bottom. White "MAGNOLIA" in upper red area with blue "GASOLINE" in center and white outlined red "FOR SALE HERE" on bottom band.

Magnolene Oils and Greases for Sale Here
15x30   (5)   1918–1925 $650
Rectangular porcelain sign with red band across top, white band in center, and blue band across bottom. White "MAGNOLENE" in upper red area with blue "MOTOR OILS AND GREASES" in center and white outlined red "FOR SALE HERE" on bottom band.

Flange Signs
Magnolene Motor Oil for Fords
16x22   (5)   1918–1925 $950
White outlined blue porcelain flange sign with white "Magnolene" script logo across upper area of sign. White "MOTOR OIL/FOR FORDS/REDUCES VIBRATION/ FOR SALE HERE" across lower sign face.

General Petroleum Corporation
Vernon, California
Identification Signs
General Gasoline & Lubricants
30"   (5)   1920–1930 $2,200
Green/white/black outlined green porcelain sign with white outlined black band diagonal across center. White "GENERAL" on band. White "GENERAL/PETROLEUM/ CORPORATION" in upper green area and "GASOLINE and LUBRICANTS" below.

Building Signs & Letters
General Gasoline w/horse
54x60   (5)   1934–1940 $850
Die-cut porcelain sign. Blue outlined flying red horse on white area with flat bottom for roofline mounting. Blue script "General" above "GASOLINE" on white area.

Pump Signs
General Gasoline & Lubricants tab
10"   (5)   1920–1925 $1,250
Green/white/black outlined green porcelain sign with white outlined black band diagonal across center. White "GENERAL" on band. White "GENERAL/PETROLEUM/CORPORATION" in upper green area and "GASOLINE and LUBRICANTS" below. Black tab for mounting to cylinder rods.

Curb Signs
General Violet Ray Anti-Knock Gasoline
30"   (5)   1925–1930 $2,800
General Violet Ray Anti-Knock Gasoline
42"   (5)   1925–1930 $2,500
Red outlined white porcelain sign with large green diamond covering most of sign face. White band across center of diamond with red outlined purple "VIOLET RAY" across center. White "GENERAL" and white outlined lightning bolt above. White outlined red "ANTI-KNOCK" below with red "GASOLINE" in white interruption of diamond near bottom.

Chek-Chart was a service provided to dealers of numerous brands of lubricants that supplied them with up-to-the-minute charts and descriptions of lubrication points on automobiles of the day. Most oil marketers subscribed to the service, and Gilmore dealers that participated in the program displayed signs like the one shown here. *Dave Mercer collection, PCM archives*

General Violet Ray Gasoline
30"   (5)   1930–1934 $2,800
Red outlined white porcelain sign with large green diamond covering most of sign face. White "GENERAL" across top over large white "VIOLET/RAY" with red and purple block drop shadow. Red "GASOLINE" in white interruption of diamond near bottom.

General Ethyl Gasoline EGC
30x30   (5)   1926–1934 $1,500
Red outlined white rounded triangular sign, point down, with red/white/green checkerboard pattern across flat top area. Green "GENERAL" above red "ETHYL/GASOLINE" across center of sign with Ethyl (EGC) logo at bottom.

Lubrication/Motor Oil Signs
Socony Certified Lubrication Service
14x20   (5)   1928–1934 $650
Blue outlined white five-point elongated white porcelain shield with blue lines around red "SOCONY/ CERTI-FIED/LUBRICATION/SERVICE CERTIFIEDÓ in blue. Blue script text below, with red outlined green General logo forming seal with blue ribbons at bottom left beside red "GENERAL PETROLEUM/CORPORATION/OF CALIFORNIA."

Mobil Certified Lubrication
14x20   (5)   1934–1946 $650
Blue outlined white five-point elongated porcelain shield with red shield outline around red "Mobil Lubrication" at top. Small blue "SOCONY VACUUM" (red horse in center) below "Mobil." Script blue "Certified" above "Lubrication." Blue script text below, with red outlined white and green General logo forming seal with blue ribbons at bottom left beside red "GENERAL PETROLEUM/CORPORATION/OF CALIFORNIA." Small flying horse and Gargoyle logos on revised seal.

White Eagle Oil and Refining
Kansas City, Missouri
Identification Signs
Gasoline White Eagle and Keynoil
42"   (5)   1925–1930 $1,250
White octagon-shaped porcelain sign with black/white outlined red octagon in center. White outlined black band across center of octagon with white "WHITE EAGLE" on band. White "GASOLINE" arched around top, "Keynoil" around bottom.

Curb Signs
Gasoline White Eagle and Keynoil
30"   4   1925–1930 $1,600
White porcelain sign with black outlined white octagon around red circle in center. White outlined black band across center of circle with white "WHITE EAGLE" on band. White "GASOLINE" arched around top, "Keynoil" around bottom.

Gasoline White Eagle and Keynoil
30"   (4)   1925–1930 $1,600
White octagon-shaped porcelain sign with red/white outlined red circle in center. White outlined black band across center of octagon with white "WHITE EAGLE" on band. White "GASOLINE" arched around top, "Keynoil" around bottom.

100% Paraffin Base Keynoil Motor Oil
30"   (5)   1920–1925 $1,250
White porcelain sign with red band across center. Black outlined white "Keynoil" on band with red and black diamond logo at top. White "PARAFFIN" on black band with white "100%" above and "BASE" below. Black "MOTOR OIL" across below red band.

Banner White Eagle Ethyl Gasoline
30"   (5)   1926–1930 $1,650
White porcelain sign with red/white outlined red circle with white center in center. Black band across center interrupted by large Ethyl (EGC) logo with yellow rays. White "WHITE EAGLE" on band. White "BANNER" arched around top, "GASOLINE" around bottom.

Lubrication/Motor Oil Signs
Keynoil strip

4x14   (5)   1920s $750

Red outlined white tin litho-embossed sign with black outlined red "Keynoil" above red line to left. Black outlined white "LUBRICATES LASTS" on line. Black outlined white octagon with black circle with red center to right. Detailed standing white eagle in center of logo with white "WHITE EAGLE" in black band across center and white "MOTOR OIL" arched above.

Vacuum Oil Company
Rochester, New York
Identification Signs
Gargoyle Mobiloil/Mobilgas

42x60   (4)   1925–1932 $750

One-sided porcelain sign faces assembled back-to-back can-style. White porcelain sign with series of progressively thicker red horizontal stripes progressing out from white band across center. Black "Mobilgas" across center band. Upper striped area is interrupted at center by 12-inch-diameter red outlined white circle, projecting above horizontal edge of sign. Red and black Gargoyle logo above black "Mobiloil" in circle.

Building Signs & Letters
Gargoyle Mobiloils Gasoline strip

18x60   (5)   1920–1925 $750

Black porcelain sign with white rectangle at left beside white "Mobilgas." White "GASOLINE" below, with red and black Gargoyle logo in white rectangle.

Curb Signs
Mobiloil Make the Chart Your Guide

24"   (5)   1920–1925 $650

Red outlined white tin litho sign with red and black Gargoyle logo at top. Black "Mobiloil" across center with black "Make the chart/your guide" below.

Ask Here for Mobiloil

28.5x32.5   (3)   1925–1930 $550

White rounded-corner square porcelain sign with red band and stripes across lower sign face. Black "Ask here for" at upper left corner above red and black Gargoyle logo above red bands. Black "Mobiloil" across red band, black "The World's Quality Oil" across bottom.

Ask Here for Gargoyle Mobiloil

24"   (1)   1920–1931 $550

White porcelain sign with black "Ask here for" across top of sign above red and black Gargoyle logo. Black "Mobiloil" below logo.

Stop Here for Gargoyle Mobiloil

24"   (1)   1931–1935 $550

Clean rest rooms were always a feature of up-to-date service stations, and Mobil dealers promoted their cleanliness with a shield-shaped pledge plaque. In later years, travelers were advised by signage to stop in the station office and pick up the key to the rest room, as they were locked for safety. *Dave Mercer collection, PCM archives*

White porcelain sign with black "Stop here/for" across top of sign above red and black Gargoyle logo. Black "Mobiloil" below logo.

Mobilgas Ethyl EGC

30"   (3)   1926–1931 $450

Red outlined white porcelain sign with Ethyl (EGC) logo with yellow rays at top. Black "Mobilgas/ETHYL" below.

Lubrication/Motor Oil Signs
Gargoyle Mobiloil vertical strip

14x60   (4)   1920s $375

Black outlined red tin litho sign with white oval at top above black outlined white vertical "MOBIL-OIL." Red and black Gargoyle logo in oval.

Drain and Refill With Gargoyle Mobiloil Now

36x60   (4)   1920–1925 $450

Red/black outlined red porcelain sign with black outlined white "Mobiloil" diagonal across center with black outlined white oval at upper left. Red and black Gargoyle logo in oval with white outlined black "Drain and refill with" across top, "NOW!" across bottom of sign.

Drain and Refill With Mobiloil
29x33   (3)   1925–1931 $400
White porcelain sign with black "Drain and Refill with–" across above red and black Gargoyle logo. Black "Mobiloil" across center above black "Make the chart your guide."

Gargoyle Mobiloil Certified Service
19.5x19.5   (4)   1926–1931 $600
White porcelain sign with irregular blue border around red outlined white center circle. Red and black Gargoyle logo at top with black "Mobiloil" across center above red "Certified Service."

Let Us Mobiloil Your Car
42x60   (3)   1925–1930 $550
White porcelain sign with irregular blue border around red outlined white center circle. Red and black Gargoyle logo at top with black "Mobiloil" across center above red "Certified Service."

Let Us Mobiloil Your Car
42x60   (3)   1925–1930 $550
Black outlined self-framed red porcelain sign with white "Mobiloil" across center. White outlined black "Let us" above "Mobiloil," "your car" below. Black outlined white "ENGINE:CHASSIS:GEARS" across bottom.

Flange Signs
Gargoyle Mobiloil flange
15.5x24   (2)   1911–1931 $750
White porcelain flange sign with black "Mobiloil" across sign face above black "VACUUM OIL COMPANY." Black outlined and detailed Gargoyle above "Mobiloil" with black "GARGOYLE" with red arched line through letter centers arched above Gargoyle figure.

Gargoyle Mobiloils A Grade...
15.5x24   (4)   1925–1930 $750
White porcelain flange sign with black "Mobiloil" across sign face above black "A grade for each type of motor." Black outlined and detailed Gargoyle above "Mobiloil" with black "GARGOYLE" with red arched line through letter centers arched above Gargoyle figure.

Gargoyle Mobiloil Make the Chart...
15.5x24   (2)   1911–1931 $750
White porcelain flange sign with black "Mobiloil" across sign face above black "Make the chart your guide." Black outlined and detailed Gargoyle above "Mobiloil" with black "GARGOYLE" with red arched line through letter centers arched above Gargoyle figure.

Lubester Signs
All of the following signs are a white/red outlined white porcelain sign with black "Mobiloil" across the center. Black outlined and detailed Gargoyle above "Mobiloil" with black "GARGOYLE" with red arched line through letter centers arched above Gargoyle figure. Black grade name below "Mobiloil." Black "Make the chart your guide" arched above Gargoyle figure. Black "This sign is the property of the Vacuum Oil Company and is loaned only on the condition that the user/guarantee to dispense from the container to which it is attached only genuine Gargoyle Mobiloil of the grade indicated." The following grade listings are known: A, ARCTIC, B, BB, E/FOR FORD CARS, and CW.

Oil Cabinet & Rack Signs
Ask for Gargoyle Mobiloil
19.5x24   (1)   1920–1929 $750
White porcelain sign with black "Ask for" across top above red and black "Gargoyle" logo. Black "Mobiloil" below logo with black "Authorized Service/VACUUM OIL COMPANY" in lower right corner.

Stop Here Gargoyle Mobiloil
19.5x24   (1)   1920–1929 $600
White porcelain sign with black "Stop here" across top above red and black "Gargoyle" logo. Black "Mobiloil" below logo with black "Authorized Service/VACUUM OIL COMPANY" in lower right corner.

Authorized Service Gargoyle Mobiloil
18x28   (5)   1920–1929 $750
Red outlined white porcelain rectangular sign with projecting area at top center. Small black "Property of/Vacuum Oil Company" in projecting area. Black "Authorized Service" across top of sign face with red script "Genuine" at left. Red and black "Gargoyle" logo in center with black "Mobiloil" below. Possibly part of an oil rack.

Ask for Gargoyle Mobiloil chart
20x40   (3)   1920–1929 $750
The often-referred-to "Mobiloil Chart," the text changed annually with automotive introductions, so exact text varies. White tin litho sign with red outline. Black "Ask for" above red and black Gargoyle logo at top. Black "Mobiloil" above "Make this chart your guide" across below "Mobiloil." Black detailed text with automobile makes and oil reference below, with black "Authorized Service/VACUUM OIL COMPANY" across bottom.

Gargoyle Mobil 30C/35C
13.5x17   (4)   1920–1929 $450
White tin litho embossed with red and black Gargoyle logo at top over black "Mobiloil." Black outlined red "30c" and "35c" below, with black text references for pricing various

grades. Red outlined white band across bottom with black "VACUUM OIL COMPANY" in band.

Lubrite Oil Company
St. Louis, Missouri
Building Signs & Letters
Lubrite station panel
12x96   (5)   1926–1930 $200
Self-framed white porcelain sign with blue "LUBRITE STATION" across panel.

Curb Signs
Vacuum Lubrite
30"   (5)   1929–1932 $475
Blue outlined white porcelain sign with red "VACUUM" across top above large red "V." Blue "Lubrite" interrupts "V" near bottom.

Wadhams Oil Corporation
Milwaukee, Wisconsin
Identification Signs
Wadhams Gasoline
48x72   (5)   1925–1936 $600
Red/yellow outlined black porcelain sign with white "Wadhams/Gasolines" across center.

Mobilgas Wadhams
48x52   (4)   1936–1942 $450
White/blue outlined white porcelain five-point shield with blue "Mobilgas" (serif "a") across center of sign face. Flying red horse with white details above "Mobilgas," with blue "WADHAMS" below "Mobilgas."

Building Signs & Letters
Wadhams panel
18x96   (5)   1925–1939 $300
Yellow outlined black porcelain sign with white "Wadhams" logotype across center.

Curb Signs
Wadhams Ethyl Gasoline
42"   (5)   1926–1930 $550
Red/white outlined black porcelain sign with red outlined white center circle. White "Wadhams" arched around top, "Gasoline" around bottom with Ethyl (EGC) logo with yellow rays in center.

Lubrication/Motor Oil Signs
Wadhams Motor Oil/Emphatically Independent
16.5x20.5   (5)   1926–1930 $1,200
Black porcelain flange sign with white "Wadhams" across top above yellow "Tempered" and white "Motor Oil." Large red circle at left center with black and yellow oil cans on circle. Small IOMA logo at right center. Series of white vertical lines across "sign" below oil cans

Longevity as a distributor or dealer was recognized by virtually every oil company and Mobil is certainly no exception. Here we see a dealer 25-year-award plaque shaped like the shield used for the Mobilgas identification sign. *Dave Mercer collection, PCM archives*

with yellow "Emphatically Independent" across bottom of sign face.

Wadhams Motor Oil/IOMA
16.5x20.5   (5)   1926–1930 $1,200
Black porcelain flange sign with white "Wadhams" across top above yellow "Tempered" and white "Motor Oil." Large red circle at left center with black and yellow oil cans on circle. Series of white vertical lines across sign below oil cans with small IOMA logo in center at bottom of sign face.

Wadhams TEMPERED Motor Oil
36x48   (4)   1915–1919 $1,100
Black/white outlined black wood framed reflective tin sign with white "Wadhams" across top and "Motor Oil" in lower right corner. Yellow "Tempered" between, with yellow and white oil can and bottle to lower left.

Secondary Signs
Wadhams True Gasoline flange
18x22   (5)   1915–1920 $1,350

Mobiloil remains a popular product overseas, even today. Oil-dispensing equipment was identified as to brand and grade by small signs such as the one we see here. *Dave Mercer collection, PCM archives*

Black porcelain sign with white flange area. White script "Wadhams" across top of sign with detailed red and black gasoline can in center. White "True/Gasoline" below can.

Wadhams Tempered Motor Oil
18x84   (5)   1920–1926 $850
Wood-framed black tin litho sign with white "Wadhams" across sign above yellow "Tempered" and white "Motor Oil." Red and white design at left with gold and white oil bottle on red circle at left.

Wadhams Tempered Motor Oil
18x84   (5)   1920–1926 $550
Black wood-framed reflective vertical tin sign with black outlined white "Wadhams" vertical down sign. Large red circle at top with yellow oil bottom over circle. Yellow "Tempered" over white "Motor/Oil" at bottom.

Wadhams Gas
18x84   (5)   1920–1926 $500
Black wood-framed reflective vertical tin sign with black outlined white "Wadhams" vertical down sign. Red square at top and bottom with black and white pump nozzle on upper square and white "Gas" diagonal on lower square.

Bulk Plant Signage
Wadhams Branch Office
48x144   (5)   1930–1939 $400

White outlined blue porcelain sign with large white "Wadhams" logotype across center. Smaller white "Branch Office" across bottom.

Bartles-McGuire Oil Co.
Milwaukee, Wisconsin
Curb Signs
Bartles Ethyl Gasoline
30"   (5)   1926–1929 $500
Black outlined light blue porcelain sign with black outlined white center circle. Large Ethyl (EGC) logo in center with black outlined yellow "BARTLES" arched around top, "GASOLINE" around bottom.

Secondary Signs
Bartles Bonded Oils and Greases
12x20   (5)   1920–1925 $650
Red/yellow outlined black embossed tin litho sign with yellow and black station attendant in uniform at left end. Yellow "Bartles" (red arrow through "B") over red "Bonded." Smaller yellow "Oils & Greases" across bottom.

White Star Refining Co.
Detroit, Michigan
Identification Signs
Staroline Gasoline is Better
36x72   (5)   1920s   No Listing
Blue tin can-type sign punched for opal glass insertion. White opal glass "Staroline" logotype over "Gasoline/IS BETTER."

White Star Gasoline/Staroleum
42"   (4)   1930–1934 $750
Blue porcelain sign with white outlined blue center circle. White "WHITE STAR" arched around top, "Gasoline" around bottom. Large white star in center with blue "STAROLEUM/MOTOR/OILS" across star.

Mobilgas White Star shield
42x48   (4)   1934–1947 $650
White/red outlined white porcelain five-point shield with blue "Mobilgas" (serif "a") across center of sign face. Flying red horse with white details above "Mobilgas," with blue circle with white star in center below "Mobilgas."

Curb Signs
Staroleum Motor Oil
30"   (5)   1924–1928 $750
Blue/white outlined blue porcelain sign with large white star border to border. Blue "Staroleum" above "MOTOR/OIL" on star.

White Star Gasoline "Staroleum"
30"   (3)   1924–1928 $750
Blue porcelain sign with white outlined blue center circle.

White "WHITE STAR" arched around top, "GASO-LINE" around bottom. Large white star in center with smaller white stars in perimeter area to either side. Blue "STAROLEUM" across center star.

White Star Gasoline blue center
30"   (4)   1918–1924 $750
Blue/white outlined blue porcelain sign with white out-lined blue center circle. Large white star in circle, with white "WHITE STAR" arched around top in blue band, "GASOLINE" below.

White Star Gasoline red center
30"   (4)   1924–1939 $800
White outlined blue porcelain sign with white outlined red center circle. Large white star in circle, with white "WHITE STAR" arched around top in blue band, "GASOLINE" below.

White Star Motor Oil red center
30"   (5)   1924–1930 $750
White outlined red porcelain sign with white outlined blue center circle. Large white star in circle, with white "WHITE STAR" arched around top, "MOTOR OIL" below.

Vacuum White Star large "V"
30"   (5)   1930–1932 $800
Blue outlined white porcelain sign with red "VACUUM" across top above large red "V." Blue "WHITE STAR" in-terrupts "V" near bottom. Blue circle with white star in center between uprights of "V."

White Star on blue, no lettering
30"   (5)   1932–1940 $450
Blue/white outlined blue porcelain sign with large white star border to border. No lettering.

Independent Oil Co. of Pennsylvania
Altoona, Pennsylvania
No signs specifically for Independent Oil are known of at this time.

Metro
Jamestown/Olean, New York
Identification Signs
Metro Gas More Power/More Mileage
30x72   (5)   1925–1930 $1,000
Red porcelain sign with large black outlined white "Metro Gas" across top above black "MORE POWER MORE MILEAGE." Black outlined white oval in center above black outlined white "Mobiloil." Small black "Ask for" at upper left of "Mobiloil." White vertical rectangle at left of lettering with red and white visible gas pump with Metro globe pictured.

Mobiloil dispensing equipment and oil can cabinets were identified with shield-shaped signs that matched the gas pump signs in the postwar years. Note the black border, indicating that is was used by Socony-Vacuum subsidiary General Petroleum on the West Coast. *Dave Mercer collection, PCM archives*

Gilmore Oil Co.
Los Angeles, California
Identification Signs
Gilmore Red Lion
48"   (5)   1932–1940   No Listing
Red outlined yellow porcelain sign with red outlined white center circle. Red and black charging lion in center circle with black outlined red "GILMORE" arched around top, "RED LION" around bottom.

Building Signs
Gilmore Gasoline
24x192   (5)   1926–1942   No Listing
Wood-framed red outlined yellow tin litho sign with black outlined "GILMORE GASOLINE" across sign. Circular "MONARCH OF ALL" signs listed below installed in the center between "GILMORE" and "GASOLINE."

Blu-Green Monarch of All
42"   (5)   1926–1933 $7,500
Red outlined yellow porcelain sign with red outlined white center circle. Orange, red, and black lion's head in center circle with black outlined red "BLU-GREEN" arched

Among the earliest signs to identify pumps that dispensed Mobilgas is this small sign from the early 1940s. Following the war, Mobilgas pumps were identified with much larger signs, die-cut in the shape of the identification shield. *Dave Mercer collection, PCM archives*

around top, "MONARCH OF ALL" around bottom. Installed in center of Gilmore Gasoline panel listed above.

Red Lion Monarch of All
42"   (5)   1933–1945 $7,500
Red outlined yellow porcelain sign with red outlined white center circle. Orange, red, and black lion's head in center circle with black outlined red "RED LION" arched around top, "MONARCH OF ALL" around bottom. Installed in center of Gilmore Gasoline panel listed above.

Rooftop Lion
42" tall   (5)   1932–1940   No Listing
Full-figure cast of standing lion for installation on station rooftops.

Gilmore Die-cut Flagman
60"   (5)   1926–1935 $4,500
Elaborate die-cut tin litho sign featuring red-and-white-suited racing flagman holding out a black-and-white checkered flag with the red Gilmore lion logo on it. Black lower panel on sign with red outlined white "Try" at top and "GASOLINE" across bottom and white outlined red "GILMORE/The RECORD/BREAKER" in center.

Neon
Gilmore strip neon
16x96   (5)   1935–1945 $2,500
Red outlined yellow porcelain sign face with black outlined red "GILMORE" across center. Faces assembled back-to-back and punched for neon "GILMORE."

Curb Signs
Gilmore Gasoline Monarch of All
18x32   (5)   1923–1925   No Listing
White porcelain vertical rectangular sign with rounded top and bottom edges. Black outlined red "GILMORE" arched across top, "GASOLINE" across bottom with black "MONARCH OF ALL" across bottom of sign. Red outlined white circle in center with black detailed orange lion head in circle.

Gilmore Record Breaker Lane
24"   (5)   1935–1939 $4,500
Yellow porcelain sign with red-and-black lion jumping across center. Red "GILMORE" logotype above lion with red "RECORD BREAKER LANE" below. Used in conjunction with Gilmore racing functions.

Lubrication/Motor Oil Signs
Gilmore Lion Head Motor Oil
12x20   (3)   1924–1930 $2,800
Yellow outlined red embossed tin litho sign with white circle in lower left corner and white band diagonal across sign up from circle. Detailed orange and black lion head in circle with black "LION HEAD" on band. Black outlined yellow "GILMORE" and small "MONARCH OF ALL" and "2000 MILES OF LUBRICATION" above band, "Motor Oil" below with white outlined black "Purest Pennsylvania" & PGCOA seal just above motor oil. Small black outlined white "THE MOST HIGHLY FILTERED/MOTOR OIL IN AMERICA" in lower right corner.

Gilmore Chek/Chart Lubrication
24x30   (5)   1932–1940 $2,200
White porcelain sign with black band across top and bottom. Black lines forming white band across center with black check mark and black "CHEK-CHART" with black outlined red "GILMORE" across top and "LUBRICATION" across bottom. Note: Chek Chart was a service of H.M. Gousha, the road map publisher. Each year Gousha published a lubrication guidebook and series of lubrication point charts for the various major oil companies. This Gilmore sign acknowledges that they indeed used this guidebook system.

Secondary Signs
Gilmore Blu-Green Gasoline
24x54   (5)   1920–1929 $3,500
Black wood-framed green tin litho sign with black outlined white "GILMORE" in upper left corner, "Gasoline" in lower right with black "BLU-GREEN" with white block drop shadow diagonal across center.

The first Mobilgas pump signs were not shield-shaped but rather had an unusual "keyhole"-shaped tin lithographed design. These signs date from the late 1930s. *Dave Mercer collection, PCM archives*

Mobilgas/Socony-Vacuum
Identification Signs

Mobilgas w/horse on rectangle
24x36   (4)   1932–1935 $500
White porcelain sign with flying red horse with white details in center at top. Blue "Mobilgas" across bottom of sign.

Mobilgas w/horse on rectangle
30x48   (4)   1932–1935 $450
White/red outlined white porcelain sign with flying red horse with white details in center at top. Blue "Mobilgas" across bottom of sign.

Mobilgas Product of a S–V Company
48x52   (4)   1932–1946 $550
White/red outlined white porcelain five-point shield with blue "Mobilgas" (serif "a") across center. Flying red horse with white details at top and red "PRODUCT OF A/SO-CONY-VACUUM /COMPANY" below "Mobilgas."

Mobilgas Socony Vacuum
48x52   (4)   1932–1946 $550
White/red outlined white porcelain five-point shield with blue "Mobilgas" (serif "a") across center. Flying red horse with white details at top and red "SOCONY-VACUUM" below "Mobilgas."

Mobilgas Socony Vacuum
48x52   (4)   1932–1946 $550
White/red outlined white porcelain five-point shield with black "Mobilgas" (serif "a") across center. Flying red horse with white details at top and red "SOCONY-VACUUM" below "Mobilgas."

Mobilgas Socony Vacuum shield
42x48   (4)   1936–1947 $550
Mobilgas Socony Vacuum shield
58x62   (3)   1936–1947 $500
Thick blue outline around a white porcelain five-point shield with blue "Mobilgas" (serif "a") across center. Blue outlined flying red horse with white details at top and red "SOCONY-VACUUM" below "Mobilgas."

Mobilgas Socony Vacuum shield
58x62   (3)   1936–1947 $500
Thick blue outline around a white porcelain five-point

Among the many products offered by Socony-Vacuum was propane (commonly called "bottle gas") for home cooking and heating use. Here we see a sign used by a distributor of Socony-Vacuum Bottle Gas. *Dave Mercer collection, PCM archives*

shield with blue "Mobilgas" (round "a") across center. Blue outlined flying red horse with white details at top and red "SOCONY-VACUUM" below "Mobilgas."

Mobilgas shield
58x62   (3)   1947–1962 $500
Thick blue outline around a white porcelain five-point shield with blue "Mobilgas" (round "a") across center. Blue outlined flying red horse with white details at top.

Mobilgas Socony-Vacuum shield
58x62   (3)   1936–1947 $500
Thick black outline around a white porcelain five-point shield with black "Mobilgas" (serif "a") across center. Black outlined flying red horse with white details at top and red "SOCONY-VACUUM" below "Mobilgas."

Mobilgas Socony-Vacuum shield
58x62   (3)   1936–1947 $500
Thick black outline around a white porcelain five-point shield with black "Mobilgas" (round "a") across center. Black outlined flying red horse with white details at top and red "SOCONY-VACUUM" below "Mobilgas."

Socony-Vacuum Aviation Products
72x72   (5)   1936–1946 $950
Red porcelain sign with white/black outlined white five-point shield covering most of sign face. Black outlined flying red horse on upper sign face with black "SOCONY-VACUUM" above red "AVIATION PRODUCTS" on lower shield area.

Building Signs & Letters
Flat Horses
Outlined as noted, flat porcelain die-cut flying red horses with white details. Known in the following sizes and styles:
29x37	White outline and details	$1,600
2 feet	Blue outlined	$1,800
3 feet	Blue outlined	$1,700
4 feet	Blue outlined	$1,500

Embossed Horses
Embossed porcelain die-cut flying red horses with white details. Known in the following sizes:
71x92	$1,500
2 feet	$1,800
3 feet	$1,700
4 feet	$1,500

Multi-piece horse facing left
48x60   (1)   1946–1966 $1,500
White outlined die-cut porcelain flying red horse with white details, facing left. Reverse channel construction with separate pieces for legs and tail.

Multi-piece horse facing right
48x60   (1)   1946–1966 $1,500
White outlined die-cut porcelain flying red horse with white details, facing right. Reverse channel construction with separate pieces for legs and tail.

Socony-Vacuum Products w/red panel
12x96   (4)   1930s $250
Red outlined white self-framed embossed porcelain strip with red "SOCONY-VACUUM PRODUCTS" across panel.

Mobilgas w/red panel
10x60   (4)   1930s $250
Red self-framed porcelain strip with black outlined white "Mobilgas" across panel.

Mobiloil w/red panel
10x60   (4)   1930s $250
Red self-framed porcelain strip with black outlined white "Mobiloil" across panel.

Mobilubrication w/red panel
10x120   (4)   1930s $250
Red self-framed porcelain strip with black outlined white "Mobilubrication" across panel.

Mobilgas blue porcelain
12" set   (3)   1946–1966 $200
Die-cut rounded embossed blue porcelain letter set spelling out "Mobilgas."

Mobiloil blue porcelain
12" set   (3)   1946–1966 $200
Die-cut rounded embossed blue porcelain letter set spelling
out "Mobiloil."

Mobilubrication blue porcelain
12" set   (3)   1946–1966 $200
Die-cut rounded embossed blue porcelain letter set spelling
out "Mobilubrication."

Pump Signs
Mobilgas Ask for Mobiloil
10x15   (3)   1939–1942 $300
White/blue outlined tin litho die-cut sign. Upper area is
rectangular with rounded corners, approximately 5x10 and
lower area is a 10-inch circle. Blue "Mobilgas" across upper
rectangle with blue "Ask for" at top of circle above flying
red horse. Blue "Mobiloil" across bottom of circle.

Mobilgas Special Ask for Mobiloil
10x15   (3)   1939–1942 $300
White/blue outlined tin litho die-cut sign. Upper area is
rectangular with rounded corners, approximately 5x10 and
lower area is a 10-inch circle. Blue "Mobilgas" above red
"SPECIAL" across upper rectangle with blue "Ask for" at
top of circle above flying red horse. Blue "Mobiloil" across
bottom of circle.

Mobilgas
5x10   (4)   1939–1942 $250
White tin litho sign with blue outline set in from edge. Red
outline shield interrupts outline at upper right corner. Red
flying horse in shield. Blue "Mobilgas" across center.

Mobilgas Special
5x10   (4)   1939–1942 $250
White tin litho sign with blue outline set in from edge. Red
outline shield interrupts outline at upper right corner. Red
flying horse in shield. Blue "Mobilgas" above red "SPE-
CIAL" across center.

Metro
5x10   (4)   1939–1942 $250
White tin litho sign with green outline set in from edge.
Red outlined black "METRO" across center.

11x12 Blue Border Shields
    All of the following are die-cut five-point shields with
a thick blue border. Blue outlined red flying horse with
white detailing at top of sign. Brand name, in sans-serif (except Mobiloil) thick-line lettering with round "a," as listed
below, appears across lower sign face below horse.

It seems far removed in this age of credit card readers in gas
pumps or even radio frequency transducers to identify customers and authorize transactions, but not so many years
ago; not every branded service station accepted credit cards
used by that brand. In rural areas, the acceptance of credit
cards was optional well into the 1950s. This sign was used to
identify those Mobilgas stations that did accept proprietary
Mobil credit cards. *Dave Mercer collection, PCM archives*

Mobiloil
11x12   (1)   1947–1954 $650
Blue serif "Mobiloil" across bottom of shield.

Blank w/horse
11x12   (5)   1947–1954 $675
Flying red horse only, no writing across bottom of shield.

Mobilgas
11x12   (1)   1947–1954 $200
Blue "Mobilgas" across bottom of shield.

Mobilgas studded
11x12   (5)   1947–1954 $200
Blue "Mobilgas" across bottom of shield. Studs welded to
back of sign for mounting on pumps. No holes in sign.

Mobilgas twin pump
7.5x7.5 5   (5)   1953–1962 $550
For use on two-product twin pumps. Blue "Mobilgas"
across bottom of shield.

Mobilgas Special
11x12   (1)   1947–1954 $200
Blue "Mobilgas" over large red "SPECIAL" across bottom
of shield.

Pump signs galore. Die-cut porcelain pump signs (or plates, as they are called in collector circles) are among Mobil's most popular images, and certainly the image with the most variations. Finding them offers many challenges for today's collector. *Dave Mercer collection, PCM archives*

Mobilgas Special studded
11x12   (5)   1947–1954 $200
Blue "Mobilgas" over large red "SPECIAL" across bottom of shield. Studs welded to back of sign for mounting on pumps. No holes in sign.

Mobilgas Special twin pump
7.5x7.5   (5)   1953–1962 $550
For use on two-product twin pumps. Blue "Mobilgas" above red "SPECIAL" across bottom of shield.

Mobilfuel Diesel
11x12   (4)   1947–1954 $400
Blue "Mobilfuel" over red "DIESEL" across bottom of shield.

Mobilgas Marine
11x12   (4)   1947–1954 $850
Blue "Mobilgas" over red "MARINE" across bottom of shield.

11"x12" White/Blue Border Shields

All of the following are die-cut five-point shields with a thin white outline around a thick blue border. Blue outlined red flying horse with white detailing at top of sign. Brand name, in sans-serif thick-line lettering with round "a," as listed below, appears across lower sign face below horse.

Mobilgas
11x12   (2)   1954–1962 $200
Blue "Mobilgas" across bottom of shield.

Mobilgas Special
11x12   (2)   1954–1962 $200
Blue "Mobilgas" over large red "SPECIAL" across bottom of sign.

Mobilfuel Diesel
11x12   (3)   1954–1962 $400
Blue "Mobilfuel" over red "DIESEL" across bottom of sign.

Mobilfuel Diesel Special
11x12   (4)   1954–1962 $550
Blue "Mobilfuel" over blue "DIESEL" over red "SPECIAL" across bottom of sign.

Mobilgas Marine
11x12   (5)   1954–1962 $850
Blue "Mobilgas" over red "MARINE" across bottom of shield.

12.5"x13" White Border Shields

All of the following are die-cut five-point shields with white edging around a thin blue (except Metro) border. Blue outlined red flying horse with white detailing at top of sign. Brand name, in sans-serif thin-line lettering with round "a,"

Socony's first expansion into West Coast gasoline operations came with the purchase of General Petroleum. General's brand and image was not superseded by anything imposed by the parent organization until well after the merger of Socony with Vacuum. Here we see an identification sign used by General in the years before the Mobilgas brand was used. *Dave Mercer collection, PCM archives*

as listed below, appears across lower sign face below horse. Used primarily in the Magnolia Mobilgas territory.

Mobilgas
12.5x13   (2)   1947–1962 $200
Blue "Mobilgas" across bottom of shield.

Mobilgas Special
12.5x13   (3)   1947–1962 $200
Blue "Mobilgas" over red "SPECIAL" across bottom of shield.

Metro
12.5x13   (3)   1947–1962 $500
Green outline and green outlined horse. Green "Metro" across bottom of shield.

Mobilfuel Diesel
12.5x13   (3)   1947–1962 $450
Blue "Mobilfuel" over red "DIESEL" across bottom of shield.

Mobilgas Marine
12.5x13   (4)   1947–1962 $850
Blue "Mobilgas" over red "MARINE" across bottom of shield.

Mobiloil products were sold out of oil merchandising cabinets installed on pump islands. The cabinets usually were identified with signage such as that shown here. *Dave Mercer collection, PCM archives*

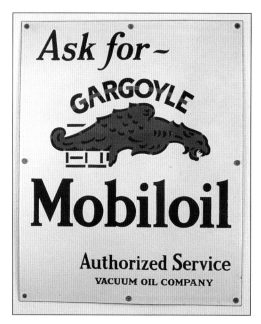

Mobilgas Aircraft
12.5x13   (4)   1947–1962 $1,400
Blue "Mobilgas" over red "AIRCRAFT" across bottom of shield.

Mobiloil Aero
12.5x13   (5)   1947–1962 $1,600
Blue "Mobiloil" over red "AERO" across bottom of shield.

11"x12" Black Border Shields

All of the following are die-cut five-point shields with a thick black border. The black border Mobilgas items were used primarily in the General Petroleum Company marketing territory on the West Coast. Black outlined red flying horse with white detailing appears at top of sign. Brand name, in sans-serif thin-line lettering with round "a," as listed below, appears across lower sign face below horse. Used primarily in the General Mobilgas territory.

Mobiloil
11x12   (2)   1947–1954 $500
Black outline/black serif letters "Mobiloil" across bottom of shield above red "SOCONY-VACUUM."

Mobiloil Socony-Vacuum (small)
7.5x7.5   (5)   1947–1954 $650
Black outline/black sans-serif letters "Mobiloil" across bottom of shield above red "SOCONY-VACUUM."

Mobiloil Socony Vacuum
11x12   (4)   1947–1954 $550
Black outline/black sans-serif letters "Mobiloil" across bottom of shield above red "SOCONY-VACUUM."

Mobilgas Socony-Vacuum
11x12   (4)   1947–1954 $500
Black outline/black "Mobilgas" across bottom of shield above red "SOCONY-VACUUM."

Mobilgas
11x12   (3)   1947–1954 $250
Black outline/black "Mobilgas" across bottom of shield above red "SOCONY-VACUUM."

Mobilgas Gasoline
11x12   (4)   1947–1954 $350
Black outline/black "Mobilgas" across bottom of shield above red "GASOLINE."

Mobilgas Special
11x12   (4)   1947–1954 $275
Black outline/black "Mobilgas" across bottom of shield above large red "SPECIAL."

Mobilgas Special Gasoline
11x12   (4)   1947–1954 $350
Black outline/black "Mobilgas" across bottom of shield above large red "SPECIAL" over smaller red "GASOLINE."

Mobilfuel Diesel
11x12   (2)   1947–1954 $525
Black outline/black "Mobilfuel" across bottom of shield above red "DIESEL."

Mobilgas Aircraft
11x12   (5)   1947–1954 $1,250
Black outline/black "Mobilgas" across bottom of shield above red "AIRCRAFT."

Mobilgas Marine
11x12   (5)   1947–1954 $950
Black outline/black "Mobilgas" across bottom of shield above red "MARINE."

11"x12" White/Blue Border Shields

All of the following are die-cut five-point shields with a thin white outline around a thick black border. Black outlined red flying horse with white detailing appears at top of sign. Brand name, in sans-serif thick-line lettering with round "a," as listed below, appears across lower sign face below horse.

Mobilgas
11x12   (2)   1954–1962 $200
Black outline/black "Mobilgas" across bottom of shield above red "SOCONY-VACUUM."

Mobilgas Gasoline
11x12   (2)   1954–1962 $250
Black outline/black "Mobilgas" across bottom of shield above red "GASOLINE."

Mobilgas Special
11x12   (2)   1954–1962 $250
Black outline/black "Mobilgas" across bottom of shield above red "SPECIAL."

Mobilgas Special Gasoline
11x12   (2)   1954–1962 $350
Black outline/black "Mobilgas" across bottom of shield above large red "SPECIAL" over smaller red "GASO-LINE."

Mobilfuel Diesel
11x12   (2)   1954–1958 $500
Black outline/black "Mobilfuel" across bottom of shield above red "DIESEL."

Mobilfuel Diesel Special
11x12   (4)   1954–1962 $650
Black outline/black "Mobilfuel" across bottom of shield above black "DIESEL" above red "SPECIAL."

Mobilgas Aircraft
11x12   (5)   1954–1962 $1,350
Black outline/black "Mobilgas" across bottom of shield above red "AIRCRAFT."

Mobilgas Marine
11x12   (5)   1954–1962 $850
Black outline/black "Mobilgas" across bottom of shield above red "MARINE."

Mobil Diesel
11x12   (2)   1958–1962 $500
Black outline/black "Mobil" across bottom of shield above red "DIESEL."

Mobil Kerosene
11x12   (2)   1958–1962 $650
Black outline/black "Mobil" across bottom of shield above red "KEROSENE."

Neon

Mobilgas w/small shield
60"   (5)   1934–1940 $850
White outlined blue porcelain faces on can-type sign. White "Mobilgas" arched across top with red outlined white five-point shield with red flying horse in shield.

Mobilgas Socony Vacuum shield
58x62   (4)   1938–1946 $850

Even the equipment used in the lubrication of automobiles carried a brand image in the 1930s and 1940s. Here we see a Mobilubrication equipment sign from the 1930s. *Dave Mercer collection, PCM archives*

Can-type porcelain sign with neon outline, horse and "Mobilgas." Thick blue outline around a white porcelain five-point shield with blue "Mobilgas" (serif "a") across center. Blue outlined flying red horse with white details at top and red "SOCONY-VACUUM" below "Mobilgas."

Mobilgas Socony Vacuum shield
58x62   (1)   1947–1962 $850
Can-type porcelain sign with neon outline, horse, and "Mobilgas." Thick blue outline around a white porcelain five-point shield with blue "Mobilgas" (round "a") across center. Blue outlined flying red horse with white details at top and red "SOCONY-VACUUM" below "Mobilgas."

Mobilgas/Mobiloil horse
72x96   (5)   1935–1940   No Listing
Elaborate die-cut formed can-type sign with wraparound two-sided face. Upper section is flying red horse leaping to outside of sign structure. Base under horse is white with white outlined blue banner diagonal under white area. White "MOBILGAS" on one side, "MOBILOIL" on the other. Red outlined black panel forming horizontal base under banner.

Pegasus
(various sizes) (3)   1935–Present $1,350
White outlined flying red horse with white details. These neon signs came in single-sided (fascia) and double-sided (rooftop) versions in many sizes by many different manufacturers. No attempt will be made to list the known varieties.

General Petroleum did not immediately adopt the Mobilgas image package that some of the other affiliates did. Here we see a General identification sign, used for rooftop mounting, that represents the beginning of the image blend between the Mobilgas horse and the General brand. *Dave Mercer collection, PCM archives*

Curb Signs

Mobilgas Product of a Socony-Vacuum Company
30"   (4)   1932–1935 $550
White/red outlined white porcelain sign with black "Mobilgas" across center. Small flying red horse above, with red "PRODUCT OF A/SOCONY-VACUUM /COMPANY" below.

Gargoyle Mobiloil Socony Vacuum
24"   (3)   1931–1938 $650
Gargoyle Mobiloil Socony Vacuum
30"   (2)   1931–1938 $600
White porcelain sign with black "Mobiloil" in serif lettering across center. Small red "SOCONY-VACUUM" below with red and black Gargoyle logo at top.

Mobiloil Socony-Vacuum
24"   (3)   1938–1946 $600
Mobiloil Socony-Vacuum
30"   (2)   1938–1946 $550

White porcelain sign with blue "Mobiloil" in serif lettering across center. Small red "SOCONY-VACUUM" below with flying red horse logo at top.

Mobiloil Marine
24"   (3)   1938–1946 $900
White porcelain sign with blue "Mobiloil" in serif lettering across center. Small red "MARINE" below with flying red horse logo at top.

Mobiloil
24"   (3)   1946–1948 $500
Mobiloil
30"   (2)   1946–1948 $450
White porcelain sign with blue "Mobiloil" in serif lettering across center.
Mobiloil Die-cut with horse
30x36   (4)   1948–1962 $400
Mobiloil Die-cut with horse
42x48   (2)   1948–1962 $375

Blue outlined white porcelain sign with white circle at top above blue strip. Large flying red horse on circle with white "Mobiloil" across strip.

Lubrication/Motor Oil Signs

Gargoyle Mobiloil shield
36x36   (5)   1932–1936 $650
Red outlined white porcelain five-point shield with red and black Gargoyle logo at top and black "Mobiloil" across center.

Gargoyle Mobiloil Socony Vacuum
36x36   (5)   1936–1940 $650
Black outlined white porcelain five-point shield with red and black Gargoyle logo at top and black "Mobiloil" across center.

Mobiloil Service shield w/horse
36x36   (5)   1954–1962 $500
Black outlined white porcelain five-point shield with flying red horse with white details at top. Black sans-serif "Mobiloil" across center with red script "Service" below.

Gargoyle Marine Oils shield
42x42   (5)   1954–1962 $850
Black outlined white porcelain five-point shield with flying red horse with white details at top. Black "Gargoyle/Marine Oils" below.

Certified Mobilubrication backbar
42x144   (5)   1940s $250
Large die-cut white tin litho sign with blue outline and blue flange trim panels. Small flying red horse at top over red script "Certified." Blue "Mobilubrication" logotype across center with red "SOCONY-VACUUM" in lower left corner.

Mobilubrication backbar
30x96   (4)   1950s $250
Blue outlined white self-framed tin litho panel with blue "Mobilubrication" across center. Small flying red horse at top.

Mobiloil World's Largest Selling Motor Oil
24x48   (3)   1950s $150
Red outlined white self-framed tin litho sign with blue "Mobiloil" across top, above blue "WORLD'S LARGEST SELLING/MOTOR OIL" across bottom.

Mobilubrication
10x26   (4)   1946–1950 $250
Red outlined white die-cut porcelain sign with blue "Mobilubrication" across center. Small flying red horse at top.

Here we see another of the many signs used to promote Mobiloil products. Motorists are reminded to consult the grade chart before adding or changing oil in their engine. *Dave Mercer collection, PCM archives*

Secondary Signs

Mobil Tires vertical panel
24x48   (3)   1946–1962 $300
Blue outlined white embossed tin litho sign. Blue "Mobil" across top. "Tires" across bottom, with flying red horse logo in center.

Shield Rest Room Pledge
7.5x7.5   (4)   1947–1962 $650
Die-cut five-point shield with thick blue line border. Blue outlined red flying horse with white detailing at top of sign.

Clean Rest Rooms octagon
16"   (2)   1958–1966 $175
Three-piece sign. Each piece is a white outlined blue porcelain flange sign designed to assemble one over the other. White "CLEAN," "REST," and "ROOMS" on individual signs.

Socony-Vacuum Credit Cards Honored Here W/B
12x18   (4)   1930–1939 $300
White porcelain sign with black "Socony-Vacuum/CREDIT CARDS/Honored Here" across sign face.

Socony-Vacuum Credit Cards Honored Here R/W/B
12x18   (3)   1938–1955 $175

Another sign displayed on cabinets from which Mobiloil products were sold is this price sign from the 1930s. *Dave Mercer collection, PCM archives*

White porcelain sign with red band across top and blue band across bottom. Blue "CREDIT CARDS" in center with white "Socony-Vacuum " in upper red area and "Honored Here" in lower blue area.

Friendly Service to Motorists
48x72   (5)   1936–1940 $175
Black outlined red self-framed tin litho sign with white stripe across bottom. Red/white/black "Mobilgas" shield diagonal at left, with white banners with black "Mobilgas" and "Mobiloil" to right. Black "FRIENDLY SERVICE TO MOTORISTS" across white stripe.

Mobiloil Marine panel w/waves
30x48   (4)   1954–1962 $700
White porcelain sign with blue "waves" that border the top and bottom. Small flying red horse at top with blue sans-serif "Mobiloil" across center. Small red "MARINE" across bottom.

Bulk Plant Signage

Marine Products Socony-Vacuum
11x11   (4)   1946–1950 $450
Die-cut five-point white tin litho shield with blue line border. Blue outlined red flying horse with white detailing at top of sign. Blue "MARINE/PRODUCTS" above red "SOCONY-VACUUM" below horse.

Mobilheat shield
13x14   (5)   1954–1962 $850
Die-cut five-point porcelain shield with blue line border. Blue outlined red flying horse with white detailing at top of sign. Blue "Mobilheat" below horse.

Correct Fuel Oil for Home Heating
6x14   (5)   1954–1962 $250
Attaches to bottom of Mobilheat shield. Red porcelain sign with white "CORRECT FUEL OIL/FOR HOME HEATING" across sign.

Mobil-Flame Bottle Gas Service
12x26   (5)   1950–1962 $2,500
White porcelain sign with blue "Mobil-flame" across sign above red "BOTTLED GAS SERVICE." Installed on hanging bracket with blue outlined red 24-inch horse above bracket.

Truck Signs

Mobilgas on red panel
10x24   (4)   1947–1954 $650
Die-cut five-point white porcelain shield with thick blue line border. Blue outlined red flying horse with white detailing at top of sign. Blue "Mobilgas" in sans-serif lettering with round "a" across lower sign face below horse. Red triangular extension to either side of shield for mounting on tank bodies at rear of truck.

Advance Signs

Just Ahead Mobilgas
48x60   (4)   1947–1958 $350
Blue self-framed tin litho sign with white/blue outlined white five-point shield in center. Flying red horse at top over blue "Mobilgas." Red "SOCONY-VACUUM" across bottom of shield. White "JUST AHEAD" above shield on blue background.

Mobil

Although the Mobil name replaced Mobilgas as the primary station identification on a gradual basis between 1955 and 1958, gasoline brands remained Mobilgas and Mobilgas Special until 1962, when they were replaced with Mobil Regular and Mobil Premium. Mobil again reimaged in 1966, replacing the elongated Mobil shield with the modern "red O" logo.

Identification Signs

Mobil
36x72   (1)   1958–1966 $175
Blue outlined white porcelain Mobil flat shield logo with red "V" forming lower outline. Small flying red horse at bottom below blue "Mobil." Blue porcelain upper frame/mounting bracket.

Mobil
36x72   (4)   1958–1966 $175
Mobil
48x96   (1)   1958–1966 $150
Blue outlined white porcelain Mobil flat shield logo with red "V" forming lower outline. Small flying red horse at bottom below blue "Mobil." Faces assembled back-to-back can-style over aluminum frame.

Mobil FRP large
48x96   (1)   1966–1980 $75
Mobil FRP small
36x72   (1)   1966–1980 $50
White fiberglass composite rectangular with rounded corners sign with white aluminum frame across top. Blue "M" and "bil" with red "o" across sign face.

Mobil FRP flat shield
36x72   (1)   1966–1980 $75
White fiberglass composite flat shield shaped sign with white aluminum frame across top. Blue "M" and "bil" with red "o" across sign face.

Building Signs & Letters

Pegasus on white circle prototype
42"   (5)   1964 Exp.   No Listing
Formed white porcelain channel-type sign with flying red horse, facing right, in center. This sign is the prototype for the plastic internally illuminated sign of the same design. It was used only in experimental locations on the "Pegasus" style station introduced in 1964.

Pump Signs

Mobil Regular
12x14   (4)   1962–1966 $75
Flat white porcelain sign with red and blue "Mobil" elongated shield across upper sign. Blue "Regular" across below logo.

Mobil Premium
12x14   (4)   1962–1966 $75
Flat white porcelain sign with red and blue "Mobil" elongated shield across upper sign. Blue "Premium" across below logo.

Mobilfuel Diesel
12x14   (4)   1962–1966 $100

The transportation of Mobilgas and Mobiloil products from refineries to terminals and on to service stations offered an excellent opportunity to advertise these same products to the motoring public simply by adding some brand-identification signage to the transport truck. Here we see an assortment of signs that appeared on Mobil trucks over the years. *Dave Mercer collection, PCM archives*

Flat white porcelain sign with red and blue "Mobil" elongated shield across upper sign. Blue "Mobilfuel/Diesel" across below logo.

Mobil Regular studded
12x14   (4)   1962–1966 $75
Embossed studded white porcelain sign with red and blue "Mobil" elongated shield across upper sign. Blue "Regular" across below logo.

Mobil Premium studded
12x14   (4)   1962–1966 $75
Embossed studded white porcelain sign with red and blue "Mobil" elongated shield across upper sign. Red "Premium" across below logo.

Mobil Diesel studded
12x14   (4)   1962–1966 $125
Embossed studded white porcelain sign with red and blue "Mobil" elongated shield across upper sign. Blue "Mobilfuel/Diesel" across below logo.

Mobil Avgas studded
12x14   (4)   1962–1966 $350
Embossed studded white porcelain sign with red and blue

While many oil companies offered automotive accessory items manufactured by national firms—Goodyear, Firestone, Exide, etc.—Mobil was one of the few companies that offered private-label TBA (tires, batteries, and accessories) under its own name. Here we have a sign from the 1950s that identified a Mobil station where Mobil-brand tires were available. *Dave Mercer collection, PCM archives*

"Mobil" elongated shield across upper sign. Blue "Avgas" across below logo with two holes drilled below for installation of grade strips.

Mobil Regular twin pump studded
6x8   (4)   1962–1966 $300
Embossed studded white porcelain sign with red and blue "Mobil" elongated shield across upper sign. Blue "Regular" across below logo.

Mobil Premium studded
6x8   (4)   1962–1966 $200
Embossed studded white porcelain sign with red and blue "Mobil" elongated shield across upper sign. Red "Premium" across below logo.

Mobil Regular
12x14   (1)   1966–1975 $75
Flat white porcelain sign with blue "Mobil" logotype (red "o") above blue "Regular" across sign.

Mobil Premium
12x14   (1)   1966–1975 $75
Flat white porcelain sign with blue "Mobil" logotype (red "o") above red "Premium" across sign.

Mobil Diesel Fuel
12x14   (2)   1966–1975 $100
Flat white porcelain sign with blue "Mobil" logotype (red "o") above black "Diesel Fuel" across sign.

Mobil Kerosene
12x14   (2)   1966–1975 $100
Flat white porcelain sign with blue "Mobil" logotype (red "o") above black "Kerosene" across sign.

Mobil Regular studded
12x14   (1)   1966–1975 $75
Embossed studded white porcelain sign with blue "Mobil" logotype (red "o") above blue "Regular" across sign.

Mobil Premium studded
12x14   (1)   1966–1975 $75
Embossed studded white porcelain sign with blue "Mobil" logotype (red "o") above red "Premium" across sign.

Mobil Diesel Fuel studded
12x14   (2)   1966–1975 $100
Embossed studded white porcelain sign with blue "Mobil" logotype (red "o") above black "Diesel Fuel" across sign.

Mobil Kerosene studded
12x14   (2)   1966–1975 $100
Embossed studded white porcelain sign with blue "Mobil" logotype (red "o") above black "Kerosene" across sign.

Mobil Marine white studded
12x14   (2)   1966–1975 $350
Embossed studded white porcelain sign with blue "Mobil" logotype (red "o") above small black "MARINE" over black outlined white "White" across sign.

Regular studded
12x14   (5)   1971–1975 $100
Embossed studded white porcelain sign with red "Regular" across center. Used at some Mobil-affiliated secondary brand stations such as "Reelo" and "Sello."

In conjunction with large signs in the service bay area, Mobil tires were displayed at curbside or on the pump islands in stands that carried the Mobil brand name as well. Here we see Mobil tire stands bearing images from the 1950s (right) and 1960s (left). *Dave Mercer collection, PCM archives*

Premium studded
12x14   (5)   1971 1975 $100
Embossed studded white porcelain sign with blue "Premium" across center. Used at some Mobil-affiliated secondary brand stations such as "Reelo" and "Sello."

Curb Signs
Mobiloil
16x30   (2)   1958–1966 $250
White rectangular porcelain sign with red "V" design from identification sign across bottom of sign. Blue "Mobiloil" across sign face above small flying red horse.

Mobilubrication
16x30   (4)   1958–1966 $250
White rectangular porcelain sign with red "V" design from identification sign across bottom of sign. Blue "Mobilubrication" across sign face above small flying red horse.

Mobil Service
16x30   (4)   1958–1966 $225
White rectangular porcelain sign with red "V" design from identification sign across bottom of sign. Blue "Mobil Service" across sign face above small flying red horse.

Secondary Signage
Mobil Credit Cards Honored
12x18   (4)   1958–1966 $150
Red outlined white tin litho sign with blue "CREDIT CARDS" across center. Red "Mobil" across top and "HONORED" across bottom.

Bulk Plant Signage
Mobil Products
16x96   (4)   1958–1966 $150
White/red outlined white porcelain strip with red/white/blue Mobil elongated shield logo at left. Blue "products" across remainder of sign.

Mobil Distributor strip
16x96   (5)   1958–1966 $150
White porcelain strip sign with red/white/blue "Mobil" flat shield logo beside blue "distributor" across strip.

Mobil Distributor square
24x36   (4)   1958–1966 $150
White porcelain sign with red/white/blue "Mobil" flat shield logo above blue "distributor."

Advance Signs
Mobil 1 Mile
48x96   (5)   1958–1966 $100
White tin litho sign with blue strip across bottom. Red/white/blue "Mobil" flat shield logo on white area with white "1 MILE" on blue strip below.

Mobil Ahead
42x84   (5)   1966–1980 $250
Black tin litho sign with white rectangle across top. Blue "M" and "bil" with red "o" across rectangle with white "ahead" below logo.

Mobiloil Cans

*w*hile as a trade name the term "Mobiloil" has passed into obscurity, no doubt it is one of the twentieth century's most frequently produced brands. As such, Mobiloil cans and other product containers remain some of the most popular among collectors. From the early years, when a fierce Gargoyle carefully guarded each can, through the "red O" era of the present, many unique and interesting designs can be found. Quite popular are the early sealed quart cans, dating from the 1934–1942 era and the earlier Gargoyle Mobiloil containers found in all sizes— and even shapes if you consider some of the Asian conical Gargoyle Mobiloil cans. Surviving quantities are significant, and an enterprising collector can easily assemble a group of 30 to 50 excellent examples. Listed herein are some of the most popular containers.

The listings in this chapter include information about the years each container was used, its size (capacity), and its price range.

Years Used

This refers to the years the item would have been sold as new stock. Many of the Mobil cans that are dated right on the can may include that date as part of the title.

Size

The liquid content measurement.

Price Range

The prices in this book are listed as a range—from wholesale to retail. Ranges are left between the two prices to allow for variations in condition, negotiation, etc. A

This collection of containers illustrates the variety of cans available to Mobil collectors. Everything from oil to polishing cloths came in tin cans.

Mobil manufactured hundreds of specialty lubricants for industrial applications worldwide. Many of the products were shipped in bulk and packaged locally, and were sold to end users in 5-gallon containers such as the one seen here. Specific lubricant information was locally stamped on the generic lithographed containers displaying the corporate image. *Dave Mercer collection, PCM archives*

Island racks were handy devices for salesmen working the driveway at Mobilgas stations. Elaborate multiple-can displays attracted motorists' attention and allowed for conversation to lead to the possible purchase of Mobil products. *Dave Mercer collection, PCM archives*

price of $1,500–2,200 simply means that $1,500 is a wholesale value and $2,200 is the top retail value. Both are considered good deals within their respective definitions.

Mobil Cans Listings

Automotive Oils in Sealed Cans
Mobiloil 100% Pure Pennsylvania Motor Oil
1934–1935   1 qt.   No Listing
Earliest sealed can. White can with thin red line forming a square "label" area on can face. Inside the "label" area is the Gargoyle trademark at the top, above black "Mobiloil." Red "100% Pure Pennsylvania" across center, above black "MOTOR OIL." Full paragraph of small black type below inside label area. Across the top of the can, above the label area, is found the motto, "Make the Mobiloil Chart Your Guide." Small black "Product of a SOCONY-VACUUM company" across bottom of can face.

Mobiloil Gargoyle Process (zigzag border)
1935–1939   1 qt./5 qt. $30–65
White can with interlocking zigzag red and black borders around top and bottom of can face. Large red and black Gargoyle logo at top of can face above black "Mobiloil." Black letter indicating grade in quotations below "Mobiloil," above small black "GARGOYLE PROCESS." Letter grades include "A," "AF," "B," "BB," "Arctic," and others.

Gargoyle Mobiloil small shield
1939–1946   1 qt./5 qt. $20–45
White can with red band around bottom. Large red and black Gargoyle logo at top of can face above black "Mobiloil." Series of thin black lines around bottom of white area interrupted at front center by small shield-shaped logo with flying red horse on shield. White "SOCONY-VACUUM OIL COMPANY, INC./MADE IN USA" on lower red band.

Mobiloil (serif lettering)
1946–1948   1 qt./5 qt. $20–45
White can with red band around bottom. Large flying red horse at top of can face above blue "Mobiloil" in thin serif lettering around center of can face. Series of thin blue lines around bottom of white area of can. White "SOCONY-VACUUM OIL COMPANY, INC./MADE IN USA" on lower red band.

Mobiloil (block lettering) Socony-Vacuum
1948–1955   1 qt./5 qt. $10–25
Solid white can with thick red band around bottom of can face. Red line around top of can face, with large flying red horse at top of can face. Light blue "Mobiloil" in tall, thin sans-serif lettering around center of can face. White "PRODUCT OF A SOCONY-VACUUM OIL COMPANY" on lower red band.

Mobiloil (block lettering) Socony Mobil
1955–1959   1 qt./5 qt. $10–25
Solid white can with thick red band around bottom of can face. Red line around top of can face, with large flying red horse at top of can face and light blue "Mobiloil" in tall, thin sans-serif lettering around center of can face. White "SOCONY MOBIL OIL COMPANY" on lower red band.

Mobiloil (block lettering) Socony Mobil
1955–1959   1 qt./5 qt. $10–25
Natural aluminum can with thick red band around bottom of can face. Red line around top of can face, with large flying red horse at top of can face and light blue "Mobiloil" in tall thin, sans-serif lettering around center of can face. White "SOCONY MOBIL OIL COMPANY" on lower red band.

Mobiloil (block lettering)
1959–1962   1 qt./5 qt. $10–25
Solid white can with thick red band around bottom of can face. Large flying red horse at top of can face and light blue "Mobiloil" in thick sans-serif lettering around center of can face. No other lettering on can face.

Mobiloil (block lettering)
1959–1962   1 qt./5 qt. $10–25

Solid natural aluminum can with thick red band around bottom of can face. Large flying red horse at top of can face and light blue "Mobiloil" in thick sans-serif lettering around center of can face. No other lettering on can face.

Mobiloil (flat shield logo)
1962–1966   1 qt./5 qt/Gal. $5–20
Manufactured in both metal and composite versions. Solid white can with band across center formed by pennants meeting point to point at the center of the can face. Blue pennant to left, red to right. The Mobil flat shield logo appears at the top of the can, with the word "Mobiloil" across the lower can face below the pennant band.

Mobiloil
1966–1970   1 qt. $5–8
Composite cans. White upper half and blue lower half. Blue "Mobiloil" (with red "O") across upper center in white area of can face. Small white slogan "WORLD FAMOUS FOR PERFORMANCE" across the bottom of the blue area.

Mobil Regular
1970–1978   1 qt. $5–8
Composite cans. Silver upper half and blue lower half. Blue "Mobil" (with red "O") across upper center in white area of can face. Small silver "regular" across below color split in blue area. Labeled "Mobiloil" on reverse in title block area.

Mobil Heavy Duty
1978–1980s   1 qt. $5–8
Composite cans. White upper half and blue lower half. Blue "Mobil" (with red "O") across upper center in white area of can face. Small white "heavy/duty" across below color split in blue area. Labeled "Mobiloil" on reverse in title block area.

Gargoyle Aero Mobiloil Blue Band
1931–1939   1 qt. $30–65
Solid white can with blue band around upper center. Red and black Gargoyle logo on upper center of can with black "Aero/Mobiloil" across lower can face. Small black "SO-CONY-VACUUM OIL COMPANY, INC./MADE IN USA" across lower edge of can face. White grade identification "BLUE/BAND" on upper color band.

Gargoyle Aero Mobiloil Green Band
1931–1939   1 qt. $30–65
Solid white can with green band around upper center. Red and black Gargoyle logo on upper center of can with black "Aero/Mobiloil" across lower can face. Small black "SO-CONY-VACUUM OIL COMPANY, INC./MADE IN USA" across lower edge of can face. White grade identification "GREEN/BAND" on upper color band.

Prior to the use of sealed cans, Mobiloil products were dispensed from bulk storage into branded bottles like these. The practice again became commonplace during the shortage years of World War II. *Dave Mercer collection, PCM archives*

Gargoyle Aero Mobiloil Gold Band
1931–1939   1 qt. $30–65
Solid white can with gold band around upper center. Red and black Gargoyle logo on upper center of can with black "Aero/Mobiloil" across lower can face. Small black "SO-CONY-VACUUM OIL COMPANY, INC./MADE IN USA" across lower edge of can face. White grade identification "GOLD/BAND" on upper color band.

Gargoyle Aero Mobiloil Gray Band
1931–1939   1 qt. $30–65
Solid white can with gray band around upper center. Red and black Gargoyle logo on upper center of can with black "Aero/Mobiloil" across lower can face. Small black "SO-CONY-VACUUM OIL COMPANY, INC./MADE IN USA" across lower edge of can face. White grade identification "GRAY/BAND" on upper color band.

Early motorists purchased motor oil in 1-quart, 2-quart, and gallon containers made of galvanized steel with lithographed panels. This rare example of Socony Motor Oil, distributed by its affiliate General Petroleum, is one of the more interesting containers that the West Coast marketing company had to offer. *Dave Mercer collection, PCM archives*

Mobiloil Aero Red Band
1939–1946   1 qt. $30–65
Solid white can with red band around lower center. Large flying horse on upper can face with slogan "FLYING HORSE POWER" arched below horse. Blue "Mobiloil/Aero" below horse and above band. White "RED BAND" on lower band.

Mobiloil Aero White Band
1939–1946   1 qt. $30–65
Solid white can with blue lines forming white band around lower center. Large flying horse on upper can face with slogan "FLYING HORSE POWER" arched below horse.

Blue "Mobiloil/Aero" below horse and above band. Blue "WHITE BAND" on lower band.

Mobiloil Aero Green Band
1939–1946   1 qt. $30–65
Solid white can with green band around lower center. Large flying horse on upper can face with slogan "FLYING HORSE POWER" arched below horse. Blue "Mobiloil/Aero" below horse and above band. White "GREEN BAND" on lower band.

Mobiloil Special
1955–1959   1 qt./5 qt. $10–25
Gold can with white band around lower third of can. Large flying red horse covers entire upper can face with blue "Mobiloil" in tall, thin sans-serif lettering over red script "Special" on white band.

Mobiloil Special
1955–1959   1 qt./5 qt. $10–25
Gold can with natural aluminum band around lower third of can. Large flying red horse covers entire upper can face with blue "Mobiloil" in tall, thin sans-serif lettering over red script "Special" on white band.

Mobiloil Special
1959–1962   1 qt./5 qt. $10–25
Gold can with white band around lower third of can. Large flying red horse covers entire upper can face with blue "Mobiloil" in thick sans-serif lettering over red script "Special" on white band.

Mobiloil Special
1959–1962   1 qt./5 qt. $10–25
Gold can with natural aluminum band around lower third of can. Large flying red horse covers entire upper can face with blue "Mobiloil" in thick sans-serif lettering over red script "Special" on white band.

Mobiloil Special
1962–1966   1 qt./5 qt/Gal. $5–20
Manufactured in both metal and composite versions. Gold upper half and white lower half can with band across center formed by pennants meeting point to point at the center of the can face. Blue pennant to left and right. The Mobil flat shield logo appears at the top of the can, with the word "Mobiloil" in blue above red "SPECIAL" across the lower can face below the pennant band.

Mobiloil Special
1966–1970   1 qt. $5–8
Composite cans. White upper half and gold lower half. Blue "Mobiloil" (with red "O") across upper center in white area of can face. White "special" across below color split in gold area.

Mobil Special 10w-30
1970–1984   1 qt. $5–8
Composite cans. White upper half and gold lower half.
Blue "Mobil" (with red "O") across upper center in white
area of can face. White outlined blue "special/10w-30"
across below color split in gold area.

Mobiloil Super
1962–1966   1 qt./5 qt/Gal. $5–20
Manufactured in both metal and composite versions. Gold
upper and lower half can with band across center formed
by pennants meeting point to point at the center of the can
face. Blue pennant to left and right, with white diamond
just below pennants. The Mobil flat shield logo appears at
the top of the can, with the word "Mobiloil" in blue across
the lower can face below the pennant band. Red "SUPER"
in white diamond area.

Mobiloil Super
1966–1970   1 qt. $5–8
Manufactured in both metal and composite versions. Solid
gold can with white line separating upper and lower halves.
Blue "Mobiloil" (with red "O") across upper center of can
face above line. White "super" across below line.

Mobil Super 10w-30
1970–1984   1 qt. $5–8
Composite cans. Solid gold can with blue line separating
upper and lower halves. Blue "Mobil" (with red "O")
across upper center in white area of can face. White outlined blue "super/10w-30" across below color split in
gold area.

Mobil Super 10w-30
1976–1984   1 qt. $5–8
Composite cans. Solid gold can with blue line separating
upper and lower halves. Blue "Mobil" (with red "O")
across upper center in white area of can face. White outlined blue "super/10w-40" across below color split in
gold area.

Mobil 1
1975–1978   1 qt. $10–12
Steel cans only. Solid silver can with large black square in
center of can face. Large numeral "1" in square, with blue
"Mobil" (with red "O") across upper area above square.
Smaller black text at bottom of can face.

Mobil 1
1978–Late 1980s 1 qt. $5–8
Steel cans only. Solid silver can with large black square in
center of can face. Large numeral "1" in square, with blue
"Mobil" (with red "O") across upper area above square.
Smaller black text at bottom of can face. Revision to text
and reverse for this later edition.

Often elaborate pyramid displays of motor oil cans were set
up on pump islands, allowing the many colors to attract customers' attention. Shown here are cans from various eras,
from the 1930s until the 1980s. *Dave Mercer collection, PCM
archives*

Vacuum's (and later Socony-Vacuum's) widely respected trademark "Mobil" was first applied to lubricants about 1904. Since that time, numerous products have borne the Mobil brand, with the most widely known being simply Mobiloil. Shown here are an assortment of product cans for Mobil's most popular products, including Mobiloil containers from the 1930s, '40s, and '50s. *Dave Mercer collection, PCM archives*

Not limited to Mobiloil alone, the Socony-Vacuum companies offered hundreds of specialty products or specific applications. Antifreeze of both permanent and methanol type, diesel engine oil, and automatic transmission fluid were just some of the many products offered under the Mobil brand. *Dave Mercer collection, PCM archives*

Prior to the merger with Socony, Vacuum Oil had purchased St. Louis–based Lubrite Oil Company, which operated gasoline stations in Missouri and Illinois and manufactured a motor oil branded simply as Lubrite. Socony-Vacuum continued to market Lubrite Motor Oil after the purchase and beyond, well into the 1970s. *Dave Mercer collection, PCM archives*

In the early years, there was little difference between automotive engine oils and aircraft engine oils. In the 1920s Vacuum introduced a premium grade motor oil called Aero Mobiloil. Although not specifically for airplanes, it was the predecessor to Mobiloil products used in later years specifically for aviation engines. Each grade was identified not with a viscosity rating, as we use today, but rather with a color band. Advertisements proclaimed "Make the Chart Your Guide," urging customers to refer to a chart posted prominently with each display of Mobiloil products so they could choose the proper oil for their engine. The early Aero Mobiloil cans contrast with the synthetic Mobil Jet Oil cans of today in this photo. *Dave Mercer collection, PCM archives*

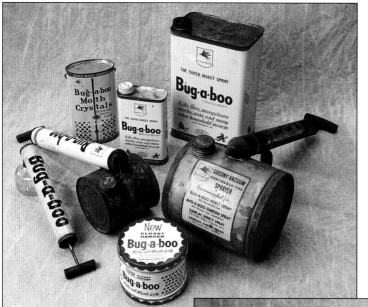

Many pest-control products were petroleum-based in the early years of this century, and many refiners developed a line of insecticides that were made from what would otherwise have been waste products. These were marketed through America's vast service station network, and Mobil was no exception. Here we see an assortment of Mobil "Bug-a-boo" products from the 1930s, '40s, and '50s. *Dave Mercer collection, PCM archives*

Although gone from the scene for many years, the fame of the red Gargoyle in representing Mobiloil products in the years before 1940 would certainly rival the representation of the flying red horse in later years. Here we see an excellent example of Gargoyle containers from the 1920s and 1930s. *Dave Mercer collection, PCM archives*

Although we are certainly more familiar with the Mobiloil products distributed by Socony-Vacuum in the United States and Canada, we are reminded that Mobil is truly an international brand name. These Asian Mobiloil cans date from the 1920s. *Dave Mercer collection, PCM archives*

Mobiloil lubricants were by no means limited to motor oils, as here we see Mobilgrease containers along with several from other companies that became part of the great Socony-Vacuum colossus. *Dave Mercer collection, PCM archives*

Automotive and aircraft engines were not the extent of Mobiloil's uses. Here we see just a small example of the many Mobiloil products that were available for marine and outboard engine use. Truly, the Mobil name has appeared on thousands of petroleum products. *Dave Mercer collection, PCM archives*

SOUTHERN
NEW ENGLAND
CONNECTICUT — MASSACHUSETTS
RHODE ISLAND

Mobil

When you travel the route of "Friendly
Service," you're never far away from a pair
of helping hands.

Almost anywhere you go, there's a Mobil
Dealer like the one "back home," with clean
rest rooms for your convenience, and expert
car care and advice for your safety.

GO MOBIL ALL THE WAY FOR
ALL YOUR TRAVEL NEEDS!

Mobil Service

Southern
New England

Connecticut
Massachusetts
Rhode Island

Mobil travel map

INLAND
No. 10
CRUISING GUIDE
THE GREAT LAKES
AND THE MISSISSIPPI RIVER

MARINE
PRODUCTS

SOCONY-VACUUM
AND
MAGNOLIA PETROLEUM CO.

MIRACLE FOLD ROAD MAP
WYOMING
and adjoining states

Sign of
Service

World's Fair
NEW YORK
1939

Mobilgas

SOCONY-VACUUM
OIL COMPANY, INC.

SO
SOCONY
MOTOR
GASOLINE

Look for this Sign

UNIFORM QUALITY
SOCONY
GASOLINE
BEST PRODUCTS

Map
of
Marked Auto Trails
in
New York

STANDARD OIL CO. OF NEW YORK
26 Broadway

MIRACLE FOLD ROAD MAP OF
THE SOUTHWEST

The Sign of
Mobilgas
...ndly Service

MAGNOLIA PETROLEUM COMPANY
A SOCONY-VACUUM COMPANY

Produced Under License From FOLDEX Limited

...Sign of
Mobilgas
...VACUUM
...PANY

Mobil Road Maps and Other Paper Items

we will make no attempt here to list Mobilgas and Mobilgas affiliate maps prior to 1939. While these maps are perhaps the most interesting, there are dozens—perhaps hundreds—of different designs related to the many divisions of the Socony-Vacuum companies prior to consolidation in 1938. Maps exist from all of the divisions: Socony, Magnolia, General, Vacuum, Wadhams, White Eagle, Lubrite, White Star, Independent, Gilmore, Metro, and others.

Mobilgas maps after 1939 display a more unified look. Major divisions of the company are consolidated, with the surviving divisions being Socony-Vacuum Oil Company, Magnolia Petroleum, and General Petroleum. Minor variations and special features, city maps, etc., are known from the divisions in the years from 1939 until all were consolidated in 1960.

Maps

Along with descriptive copy, the following information appears for each map or printed item listed in this section:

Map Title: This is simply the Mobilgas identification name for the map style (i.e.: Mobilgas Touring Map).

Official Date: Most common Mobilgas maps carry a publisher's date or date code.

Price Range: This is the price or price range in which this map is commonly traded in collector circles. The lower end pricing is considered wholesale, among dealers, while the upper end is considered retail, to the end owner. Both are considered good deals within their respective definitions.

With their vivid colors and beautiful cover art, Mobil road maps are fast becoming hot collectibles. These maps date from the 1920s to the 1980s.

Mobil offered a free travel service for customers, along with free road maps displayed in racks like this one that hung conveniently in every service station office. *Dave Mercer collection, PCM archives*

1939

For 1939, maps distributed in the former Socony marketing area display the Mobilgas brand name for the first time. Maps for 1939, as a general rule, display a two–panel cover. The front cover has a white border area around a red lower third and a two-tone blue upper two-thirds, with the blue depicting clouds in the sky. A line drawing of a Mobilgas shield sign and pole project from the lower red area up into the sky area. The rear panel shows small drawings discussing features of the map. Maps are produced by General Drafting Company.

Value for Most Titles: $5–8

Along with regular road maps, Mobil offered numerous specialty maps including marine "Cruising Guide" charts, World's Fair maps, and many other unusual paper handout items. *Dave Mercer collection, PCM archives*

1940

For 1940, Mobilgas maps show a real duotone photo of a highway scene, in shades of blue, on the lower area of the map cover. The upper third is red and the Mobilgas shield sign and pole shown project from a blue circle in the upper center of the map. The rear panel shows small drawings discussing features of the map. Maps are produced by General Drafting Company.

Value for Most Titles: $5–8

1941

The 1941 Mobilgas maps are significantly different than their predecessors. Again, the typical example is a two-panel map; however, the predominant red cover has been replaced by a two-tone blue cover, with the center area, in an aqua blue, covered with multiple images of the flying red horse. A single large Mobilgas shield is displayed in the center. Dark blue bands at the top and bot-

tom list the title (top) and corporate information (bottom). Safety tips similar to those used on Kyso maps in the early 1950s are on the back. Maps are produced by General Drafting Company.

Value for Most Titles: $6–10

1942

Mobilgas maps for 1942 are essentially identical to the 1941 maps, except the vivid tones are gone, and a dull gray-blue replaces the brilliant aqua of the previous year. This is one of the rarest years of all Mobilgas maps. Maps are produced by General Drafting Company.

Value for Most Titles: $10–15

1946–1949

Mobilgas maps for these years are all essentially the same. They feature two essentially identical panels, with a white outline around an otherwise solid red cover. The center of the cover displays a large Mobilgas shield. Titles are in white at the top, and a blue and white oval line drawing showing a car and highway scene runs below the shield. White lettering reading "TRAVEL THE ROUTE OF FRIENDLY SERVICE" appears around the oval. Maps are produced by Rand McNally.

Value for Most Titles: $10–15

1950–1955

All of the maps in this era are virtually identical. They are titled as "Miracle Fold Road Maps" after a special accordion fold design that was developed for the General Petroleum division in the late 1940s. A white outline with a blue band across the top runs across the cover; the remainder of the cover is red. The map title is in white in the blue area. The red section features a large Mobilgas shield with the motto in white script "Travel the Route of Friendly Service."

The corporate division, whether Socony-Vacuum, Magnolia Petroleum, or General Petroleum, is listed in blue across the bottom. The reverse is similar in design, with small "Mobilgas-Mobiloil" logos at the color split and a list of some Mobil products in the red area below. Maps are produced by Rand McNally.

Value for Most Titles: $8–12

1956

These maps are identical to the 1950–1955 maps, except for the new corporate identification "Socony Mobil Oil Company."

Value for Most Titles: $8–12

1957

Similar to the 1956 issue, except the new Mobil flat shield logo appears near the bottom of the front cover. Replacing the Mobilgas-Mobiloil logos on the reverse is an advertisement for Mobil credit cards. Maps are produced by Rand McNally.

Value for Most Titles: $8–12

1958

Similar to the 1957 issue, except the new Mobil flat shield logo replaces the older large Mobilgas shield. Maps are produced by Rand McNally.

Value for Most Titles: $10–15

1959

For 1959 Mobil adopted an entirely new design. The entire cover became a scenic line drawing of a Mobil service station, with the predominant colors being shades of blue for the sky and clouds. A large Mobil flat shield is located at the top, with text noting travel services below.

On maps from all parts of the country except the Southwest, the reverse features a full panel on Mobil credit cards, and the dual logo card is pictured at the top. For maps

One of the first road maps offered by any of the Socony-Vacuum companies is this Socony map from the early 1920s. *Dave Mercer collection, PCM archives*

of states in the Southwest, the first advertisements for Mobil Travel Guides appeared. (See more on the Mobil Travel Guides below.) Maps are produced by Rand McNally.

Value for Most Titles: $6–10

1960

The 1959 cover design was used again in 1960, with changes primarily on the reverse. On maps from all parts of the country except the Southwest, the credit card advertisement continued, this time showing the card that displays an entire service station scene. For maps of states in the Southwest, a redesigned advertisement for Mobil Travel Guides appeared. (See more on the Mobil Travel Guides below.) Maps are produced by Rand McNally.

Value for Most Titles: $6–10

1961

For 1961, Mobil maps featured a busy station scene on the cover. It showed a portion of the red and white porcelain station along with an island scene with attendants fueling cars. The predominant colors are shades of blue for the sky and clouds. A large Mobil flat shield is located at the top, with text noting travel services below. Note that the pumps display the shield-shaped pump signs.

Mobil jobbers and dealers sponsored many local promotions of all kinds. Here we see advertising items from several of these promotions. *Dave Mercer collection, PCM archives*

On maps from all parts of the country except those where Mobil Travel Guides were available, the reverse featured a full panel on Mobil credit cards, and the station scene card is pictured at the top. For maps of states in the areas where the travel guides were available, advertisements for Mobil Travel Guides appeared. (See more on the Mobil Travel Guides below.) Maps are produced by Rand McNally.

Value for Most Titles: $6–10

1962 & 1963

Maps for these years are virtually identical to the 1961 maps, with two exceptions: The two pumps on the cover now feature the flat shield logo on the lower pump doors, and the reverse covers show an array of Mobil Travel Guides, which were now available nationwide. Maps are produced by Rand McNally.

Value for Most Titles: $5–8

1964

The front cover of the 1964 Mobil maps features a scene similar to that of 1961–1963, except that the station shown is the new blue and white porcelain design and the cars are newer. The pumps feature drawings of the actual Mobil Regular and Mobil Premium pump plates. Ads for the Mobil Travel Guides continue on the reverse. Maps are produced by Rand McNally.

Value for Most Titles: $5–8

1965

Mobil maps for 1965 featured a design that was a significant deviation from the prior years. On the cover is an actual photo of a couple in a convertible being shown the advantages of the Mobil Travel Guide by a service station dealer. The predominant color is sky blue, with a white band at the top and white around the sides. The Mobil flat shield logo with black features is positioned at the top of the photo, with the title in black, above.

On the reverse is a smaller but similar photo and information on the Mobil Travel Guides. Maps are produced by Rand McNally.

Value for Most Titles: $3–5

1966–1974

Mobil maps changed radically for 1966. With the 1966 issues, Mobil incorporated its new "red O" look for the Mobil logo into its maps. The map cover is solid white, with a black box on the lower third of the cover. Inside the black box are three rows of three circles, each circle displaying the flying horse logo in a style similar to the new station signage. Just above the box is the heading "Mobil (in color) travel map (in black)" The rest of the upper map is solid white except for the title, in black, in the upper left corner.

The entire reverse is dedicated to advertisements for the Mobil Travel Guides. Each year in this series features a slightly different design or color of travel guide and most have a date shown with the travel guide, so that the maps are easily dated. Maps are produced by Rand McNally.

Value for Most Titles $2–4

1975

Typical of the gas shortage years and the waning days of the free road map, the 1975 Mobil maps are identical in design to the 1966–1974 maps except that they are only about two–thirds the physical size, a most interesting variation. Maps are produced by Rand McNally.

Value for Most Titles $3–5

1980s

In the mid-1980s, Mobil again offered a branded road map, this time for sale. The cover featured an abstract, diffused car and highway scene. Cover colors are pastels, and several different colors are known.

Value for Most Titles $5–8

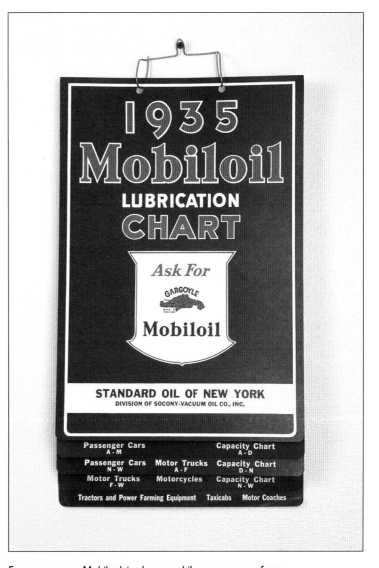

For many years Mobil advised automobile owners to refer to a grade chart in choosing the correct motor oils. Here we see an example of the 1935 Mobiloil chart. *Dave Mercer collection, PCM archives*

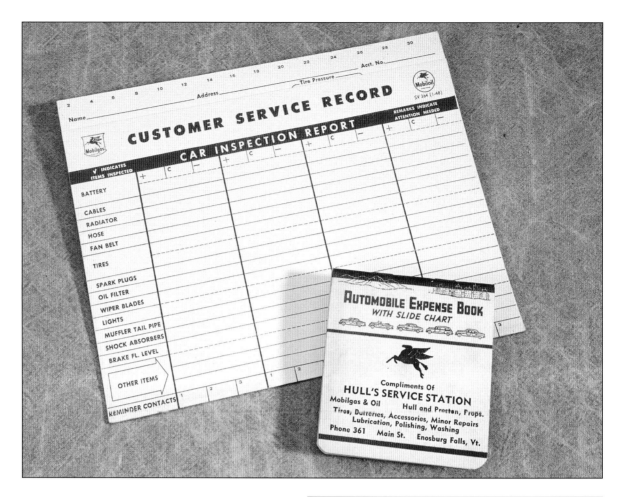

Since we live in an age of convenience stores it may seem unusual that service station dealers reaped much of their profit from a repetitive business in automotive lubrication, but they did. Here we see a Mobiloil service record that allowed a dealer to track a customer's driving and buying habits and call him when it was time for automotive service. *Dave Mercer collection, PCM archives*

Postcard advertisements were used by service station dealers as part of their service reminder program, and many were distributed with credit card statements. Here we see an assortment used by the Socony-Vacuum companies over the years. *Dave Mercer collection, PCM archives*

Advertising pennants proudly display the famed Gilmore logos of the 1930s. Gilmore was one of the more image-minded gasoline marketers of all time, and its lion has adorned advertising items of all kinds. *Dave Mercer collection, PCM archives*

Staples of a well-equipped Mobilgas station included this credit card imprinter, file box for service records, and product order reminder and note holder. *Dave Mercer collection, PCM archives*

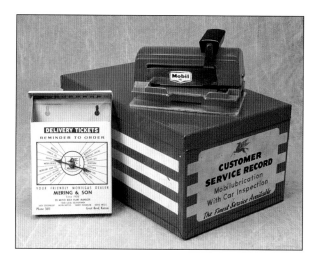

Ever popular with service station dealers were imprinted match covers. Here we see a number of stock designs used by Mobil jobbers and dealers over the years. *Dave Mercer collection, PCM archives*

Above, left

Fuel transportation is inherently dangerous, much more so than transportation of general commodities. Every oil company recognizes the achievements of its safety-conscious transport driver fleet. Here we see several driver award identification cards. *Dave Mercer collection, PCM archives*

Above

Credit cards have been used as a patronage tool by the oil companies since the 1920s. Here we have examples of the many Mobil-branded cards used over the years. Note the early paper card and the dual-logo plastic card used in the late 1950s. *Dave Mercer collection, PCM archives*

Seasonal reminders for automotive services often included cartoon drawings of weather-related images all designed to encourage automotive owners to stop by for much-needed services. *Dave Mercer collection, PCM archives*

chapter eight ···

Mobil Toys

his will perhaps be the shortest chapter in this book, not because there are few Mobil toys but rather because there are so many that it is impossible to classify them.

Many gasoline marketers were either so limited in geographic scope that toys bearing their brand names would have had limited popularity; others would not allow the reproduction of their trademarks. For such marketers, there are few examples of toys bearing their name and image.

Not so with Mobil, a worldwide marketer. The Mobil name and flying horse trademark were as familiar to children in Winston-Salem, North Carolina, as to those in Windsor, Ontario, or Westminster, Great Britain. In fact, many of the known Mobil toys were tin lithographed stations and toy trucks that were made in Europe for worldwide markets. Listed below are just a few of the hundreds of Mobil items.

White 3000 Series Tanker
1950s   No Price Listing
Tin litho truck with tank having a solid red cab with a black chassis and a red-over-white tank trailer. Black outlined white "Mobil" and "gas" along sides of tanker, with Mobilgas shield and horse interrupting between words. Truck is patterned loosely after the 1949 series White 3000 cab-over trucks.

White 3000 Series Tanker
1950s   No Listing
Tin litho truck with tank having solid red cab with black chassis and red-over-white tank trailer. Black outlined white "Mobil" and "oil" along sides of tanker, with Mobilgas shield and horse interrupting between words. Truck

is patterned loosely after the 1949 series White 3000 cab-over trucks.

White 3000 Series Tanker
1960s   No Listing
Tin litho truck with tank having solid red cab with black chassis and white-over-red tank trailer. Black "Mobil" and "gas" along sides of tanker, with Mobilgas shield and horse interrupting between words. Truck is patterned after the 1949 series White 3000 cab-over trucks.

White 3000 Series Tanker
1960s   No Listing
Tin litho truck with tank having solid red cab with black chassis and red tank trailer with white panel on sides. Black "Mobilgas" along sides of tanker. Flat shield logo on rear of tanker. Truck is patterned loosely after the 1949 series White 3000 cab-over trucks.

Transport Truck
1950s   No Listing
Tin litho tractor and tank trailer-style transport truck having solid red cab with black chassis and red-over-white tank trailer. White outlined black "Mobil" and "gas" along sides of tanker, with Mobilgas shield and horse interrupting between words.

GMC Tanker
1950s   No Listing
Tin litho tractor and tank trailer-style transport truck having blue lower half and white upper half. Tank sides display "GASOLINE" in red, but each end of the tank features the flying red horse. Cab appears to be a GMC.

Mobil was one of the more liberal companies in allowing its name and image to be displayed on generic toys. These Mobiloil tin litho trucks date from the 1950s and 1960s. *Dave Mercer collection, PCM archives*

Although certainly not a toy, this modern miniature is an excellent replica of the Mobilgas drum station of the 1940s. *Dave Mercer collection, PCM archives*

Popular among collectors today are the "fat-man" banks of the 1940s and '50s. Shown here is the Mobilgas attendant version, although many others are known. *Dave Mercer collection, PCM archives*

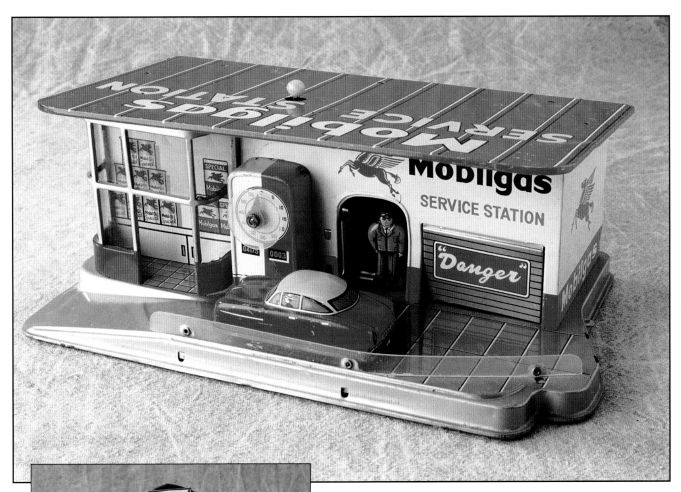

Many European toy manufacturers used the Mobil image on their toy stations as well. Here we see a tin litho replica of a European Mobilgas station. *Dave Mercer collection, PCM archives*

Service station attendant uniforms have long been popular collectibles, although here we see a miniature Mobilgas station attendant uniform on a doll. *Dave Mercer collection, PCM archives*

Mobil Trinkets and Other Small Items

he Mobil name and flying red horse have appeared on countless items. This area provides the Mobil collector with the most variety and affordability, as many objects can be bought for under $100. This chapter illustrates just some of the many trinkets that are available.

These items were supplied by Mobil to promote specific products, usually upon introduction, or given to dealers as prizes for specific product sales achievements. Items such as the radios had multiple purposes, as they could be sold, given to favored customers as gifts, or used as dealer or station employee incentives.

Company-Supplied Trinkets: Radios

Mobil 1 Synthetic Motor Oil radio
1975 promotional radio in the shape of a "Mobil 1" oil can. Price range: $40–50

Approved Trinkets

Though not supplied directly by Mobil, nor used in conjunction with a particular promotion or product introduction, these items are considered highly collectible today. Manufactured by independent advertising companies and sold through Mobil distributor representatives to independent distributors, these items are often custom imprinted for the dealer or distributor that used them in his own promotions, often tied into station openings or given to heating oil customers as Christmas gifts.

Some of these listings include dates the items were available, rarity ratings, and a price range. (Rarity and price use the same standards as detailed in the globes and signs sections.)

Gas Pump Salt & Pepper Shaker Sets

Mobilgas and Mobilgas Special
Pre-1955   (1) $50–100
Cast red plastic salt shaker labeled in the image of a Mobilgas Martin & Schwartz Model 80 gas pump and a cast red and white plastic salt shaker labeled in the image of a Mobilgas Special Martin & Schwartz Model 80 gas pump.

Sign Pole Thermometers

Sign pole thermometers were manufactured by Nationwide Advertising Company of Arlington, Texas, and were labeled with the images of virtually every oil company. Individual distributors could buy them with a custom message printed on the base. Mobil distributors, of course, were offered this promotion, and many used the thermometers as a gift to their heating oil customers.

Mobilgas shield sign
1950–1958   2 $25–35
Sign pole thermometer with the image of the classic Mobilgas shield. Custom imprint for local distributors appeared on the pole base.

Mobil flat shield sign
1958–1966   3 $25–35
Sign pole thermometer with the image of the newer Mobilgas "flat shield." Custom imprint for local distributors appeared on the pole base.

Pens and Pencils

No attempt will be made to list the thousands of types of writing instruments to which the Mobil logo has been applied. On the corporate level, many high-quality pen sets were used as employee incentives, while on the other end, Mobil distributors were free to purchase pens

---

One of the most popular advertising items of all times were salt and pepper shakers designed in the shape of gas pumps and bearing the image of each company's designs. Shown here are Mobilgas and Mobilgas Special shakers in the shape of Martin and Schwartz Model 80 pumps. Price range: $25–50
Dave Mercer collection, PCM archives

Even lubrication service attendants displayed the corporate image in their work. This is one of the more elaborate attendant hats ever used by a major oil company. Price range: $50–150 *Dave Mercer collection, PCM archives*

Shown here is an assortment of attendant hats used by Mobil service attendants over the years. Price range: $50–150 *Dave Mercer collection, PCM archives*

Achievements and years of service are always rewarded in major corporations, and Mobil was no exception. Shown here are a number of award trophies used by Socony-Vacuum. Price range: $50–250 *Dave Mercer collection, PCM archives*

from advertising companies and have their custom graphics applied. The "local" nature of some of these makes them very popular with collectors at a local or regional level.

Employee-Related Items Uniforms

Among the many Mobilgas items that have found popularity with collectors of petroleum memorabilia in recent years are Mobilgas attendant uniforms. Perhaps most personally identifying Mobilgas service to the motoring public, Mobil attendants at retail stations were attired in a uniform that implied that the attendant was an authority in meeting the needs of the motoring public. Several uniform styles are known, although no attempt will be made here to describe them. Also popular are Mobil attendant hats, particularly the "lubritorium" hats, collectible all on their own. Several styles are shown. Price range: $175–250

Patches

A part of every Mobil uniform were logo patches. Embroidered emblems representing the Mobilgas trademarks and special promotional patches were available in assorted sizes for use on shirt pocket, sleeve, hat, or shirt back. All

are highly collectible, although most are commonly found and are available in the $3–10 range. Price range: $5–25

Badges

Prior to the use of embroidered patches, Mobil uniforms included identification badges in several styles. Often these badges were made of stamped brass, inlaid with enamel colors, and die cut in the shape of the Mobilgas shield. Several designs are known, all very popular among collectors. Some were used as early attendant patches, others as employee passes to corporate facility premises. Price range: $325–500

Dishes

There are known to be dishes, glassware, and flatware bearing the Mobil trademark, found mostly in areas where Mobil operated manufacturing facilities. Employee lunchrooms at refineries, lubricants blending plants, offshore drilling platforms, and ocean-going tanker ships were the sources of these rare and valuable items. No attempt will be made to list them, but several styles are available with various logos used through the years shown. Price range: $75–250 per piece.

Ever promotion-minded, Gilmore used advertising novelties of every kind to hold the interest of customers. Here we see an assortment of Gilmore items from the 1920s and '30s. Price range: $20–500 *Dave Mercer collection, PCM archives*

Left
Mobil is a popular company for collectibles, particularly among former employees and dealers/jobbers. Such a following has made possible the manufacture of a number of nostalgia items displaying the Mobilgas image. Here we see two replica gas pumps. The one on the right is a telephone in disguise. Price range: $20–75 *Dave Mercer collection, PCM archives*

Desert motorists carried water in canvas bags strapped to the front of their automobiles for emergency use. Air current passing through the bag kept the water cool in even the hottest ambient temperatures. Here we see a desert water bag that carries the Mobilgas shield logo. Price range: $25–50 *Dave Mercer collection, PCM archives*

Battery service was an important part of a Mobil dealer's stock in trade. Here we see several of the tools required for testing automobile batteries. Price range: $100–200 *Dave Mercer collection, PCM archives*

The patriotic seal that was attached to the desert travel water bag. *Dave Mercer collection, PCM archives*

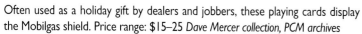

Often used as a holiday gift by dealers and jobbers, these playing cards display the Mobilgas shield. Price range: $15–25 *Dave Mercer collection, PCM archives*

Another modern "replica" item is this novelty motor oil container made in the image of the Mobil 1 Synthetic Oil can that was introduced in 1975. Price range: $15–25 *Dave Mercer collection, PCM archives*

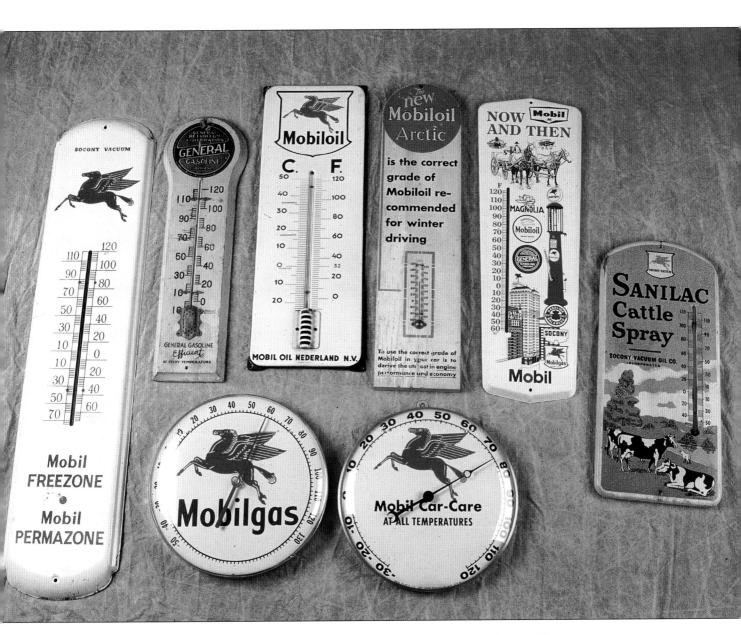

Advertising thermometers have always been popular, and Mobil has used a number of them over the years. This assortment dates from the 1920s to today. Price range: $100–500 *Dave Mercer collection, PCM archives*

Civic-minded Mobil dealers were often involved in local promotions. This Mobil dealer advertised at the ballpark on this unique display scoreboard. No price listing. *Dave Mercer collection, PCM archives*

Long before the static-sticking vinyl oil change reminders of the present, oil marketers used die-cut embossed tags that attached to the oil dip stick. They were marked with oil change mileage and served as a reminder for service station attendants to check your oil and in turn sell you an oil change. No price listing. *Dave Mercer collection, PCM archives*

Mobil dealers occasionally offered drinking glasses tied to a particular promotion. Thses two glasses date to the late 1940s. Price range: $10–25 *Dave Mercer collection, PCM archives*

These Mobilgas drinking glasses from the 1960s shed the wonderful artistic images of the earlier glasses. Price range: $10–25 *Dave Mercer collection, PCM archives*

Socony-Vacuum offered a line of candles known as "Tavern" brand candles. This an elaborate display of Socony-Vacuum "Tavern" candles includes reindeer and snowman figures that were sold at Christmas time. Price range: $25–100 *Dave Mercer collection, PCM archives*

Employees often were allowed access to company property only when wearing identification badges and pins. These Mobil pins illustrate how the design has changed over the years. Price range: $100 and up *Dave Mercer collection, PCM archives*

Mobil tie pins were popular with employees of yesterday and collectors of today. Price range: $50 and up *Dave Mercer collection, PCM archives*

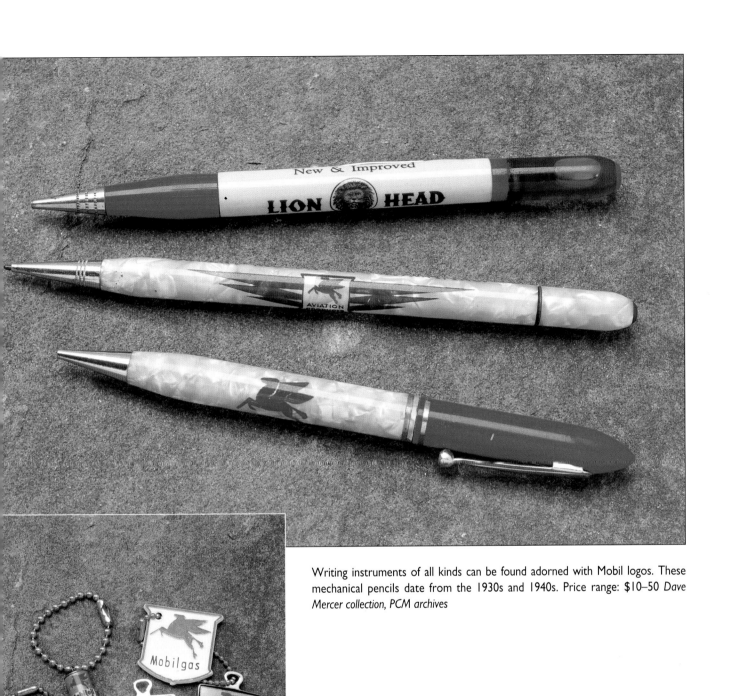

Writing instruments of all kinds can be found adorned with Mobil logos. These mechanical pencils date from the 1930s and 1940s. Price range: $10–50 *Dave Mercer collection, PCM archives*

Although key chains were a common advertising tool during most of this century, these Mobil key chains are quite rare. Even rarer are the keys with the ends shaped and cast in the image of Mobil logos. Price range: $10–50 *Dave Mercer collection, PCM archives*

113

Belt buckles for dealer uniforms or employee awards all feature the flying horse logo. Price range: $25 and up

Similar in use to the safe-driving awards given to transport drivers, these safety and service award pins were given for employee service recognition over the years. Due to the sometimes sentimental nature of this type of collectible, they can be quite rare and valuable. Price range: $100 and up *Dave Mercer collection, PCM archives*

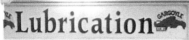

Advertising cigarette lighters were another employee or dealer incentive award used for many years. Here we see several lighters bearing Mobil images, including one given to employees in the paint-manufacturing division.

Previous page
Collector interest has developed a market for fantasy items of all kinds, and custom models are certainly among the most interesting. Here we see two scenes showing a model Mobilgas station as an exact replica of how a highway station of the late 1920s might have looked. No price listing. *Dave Mercer collection, PCM archives*

During the 1930s and 1940s, the Mobilgas flying red horse design appeared on numerous license plate attachments. Shown here are several examples. Price range: $50 and up *Dave Mercer collection, PCM archives*

Pin-back buttons were just one of the many advertising tools used by Mobil over the years. Here we see an assortment from the 1920s through the 1980s. Price range: $25–500 *Dave Mercer collection, PCM archives*

This electric clock advertised Mobiloil products and displayed the can used in the late 1930s. Price range: $150–300 *Dave Mercer collection, PCM archives*

Numerous devices have been used through the years to remind motorists of the proper time to change the oil in their engine. Lubrication reminders have been designed to hang on dipsticks, clip to sun visors, stick to door posts, and today there are even stickers that stick to the upper windshield. Shown here are various reminder devices used by Mobil and predecessor companies through the years. Price range: $3–25 *Dave Mercer collection, PCM archives*

This Mobil station clock was more general in its advertising scope and displayed only the flying red horse. It dates from the 1950s. Price range: $150–300 *Dave Mercer collection, PCM archives*

Here's a rare item! Mobil station rest rooms had hand soap dispensers that displayed the ubiquitous flying red horse. No listing. *Dave Mercer collection, PCM archives*

One of the more unusual items to display the Mobil image is this device designed to measure tire tread depth. Price range: $25–50 *Dave Mercer collection, PCM archives*

Mobil Gas Pump Color Schemes

he same diversity that we have seen in many of the Mobil items is reflected in the choice for pump color schemes among the various Mobilgas divisions. No central standard existed for pump colors, or even for grade names.

The listing below is a cross section of pumps used by marketing divisions in the East and Upper Midwest. Designs used in the Magnolia, General Petroleum, Wadhams, and White Eagle territories vary greatly from the listings below. Image standards consolidated after World War II, and in this era Socony-Vacuum was a partial owner of the Martin and Schwartz pump company. Martin and Schwartz Model 80 script top pumps were used almost exclusively in this era. Following the withdrawal of Mobil from the Martin and Schwartz operation, all makes of pumps were used until 1966, although the Model 80s were found in common usage for many years.

In 1966 Mobil reimaged (see station designs), and part of the reimaging included a custom-designed pump. Manufactured by Gilbarco, this pump featured custom cabinetry on a standard Trimline frame. The lower doors were made of stainless steel or brushed aluminum and the pump was in the shape of an oil drum. Most Mobil sta-

From the late 1930s until after World War II, Socony-Vacuum, along with Sun Oil, Continental Oil, and Standard Oil Company of Indiana owned the well-known gas pump manufacturer Martin and Schwartz. The Martin and Schwartz Model 80 was custom designed for use by the owner companies, and here we see the Mobilgas version of the Model 80, often referred to as the "script top." The top housing of the pump was die-punched to allow the installation of a plastic panel formed to show the lettering "Mobilgas" or "Mobilgas Special." This restoration captures the image of the Mobilgas script top pump perfectly. *Dave Mercer collection, PCM archives*

tions adopted this style of pump for use over the next 20 years until electronic pumps and MPDs came into common usage.

Socony

Regular 1915–1932: Socony Gasoline
Solid red pump. Small "Use Socony Motor Oil" sign attached to lower pump door. Pumps occasionally had decals for special promotions. Grade identification by globe.

Premium 1922–1927: Socony Special
Red pump with white upper half. Small "Use Socony Motor Oil" sign attached to lower pump door. Pumps occasionally had decals for special promotions. Grade identification by globe.

Premium 1927–1932: Socony Ethyl
Red pump with white upper half. Small "Use Socony Motor Oil" sign attached to lower pump door. Pumps occasionally had decals for special promotions. Grade identification by globe.

Vacuum

Regular 1926–1932: Vacuum Mobilgas
Solid white pump with a 12-inch red band around the base. Pumps occasionally had decals for special promotions. Grade identification by globe or ad panel.

Premium 1926–1932: Vacuum Mobilgas Ethyl
Solid white pump with a 12-inch red band around the base. Pumps occasionally had decals for special promotions. Grade identification by globe or ad panel.

Mobilgas—The Early Years

Regular 1932–1946: Mobilgas
Solid red pump. Decal design varied by division, but decals were used until about 1940, when small round tin litho "Mobilgas/Ask for Mobiloil" signs or small rectangular

"Mobilgas" signs were added to the lower doors.

Premium 1932–1936: Mobilgas Ethyl
Red pump with white upper half. Decal design varied by division.

Premium 1936–1946: Mobilgas Special
Red pump with white upper half. Decal design varied by division, but decals were used until about 1940 when small round tin litho "Mobilgas/Ask for Mobiloil" signs or small rectangular "Mobilgas / SPECIAL" signs were added to the lower doors.

Mobilgas—Image Consolidation

Regular 1946–1962: Mobilgas
Solid red pump. Most pump styles used featured ad glass panels. In the 1940s and 1950s, Mobil used Martin and Schwartz Model 80 script top pumps with white Mobilgas letters at the top. A porcelain "Mobilgas" shield-shaped pump sign (or rarely, a decal) was attached to the pump door approximately 8 inches below the dial glass window.

Premium 1946–1962: Mobilgas Special
Pump sides and top were painted red with white doors on either face. Most pump styles used featured ad glass panels. In the 1940s and 1950s, Mobil used Martin and Schwartz Model 80 script top pumps with white Mobilgas letters at the top. A porcelain "Mobilgas" shield-shaped pump sign (or rarely, a decal) was attached to the pump door approximately 8 inches below the dial glass window.

Mobilgas—The Mobil Years

Regular 1962–1966: Mobil Regular
Solid red pump in painted areas (although chrome was becoming more common for upper pump housings). Most pump styles that were used featured ad glass panels. A porcelain "Mobil Regular" rectangular pump sign (drilled or studded) was attached to the pump door approximately 8 inches below the dial glass window.

Premium 1962–1966: Mobil Premium
Solid white pump in painted areas (although chrome was becoming more common for upper pump housings). Most pump styles that were used featured ad glass panels. A porcelain "Mobil Premium" rectangular pump sign (drilled or studded) was attached to the pump door approximately 8 inches below the dial glass window.

INDEX